PRACTICAL SQL MASTERING DATABASE QUERIES AND MANAGEMENT

A Beginner's Guide to SQL Queries, Data Management, and Reporting

THOMPSON CARTER

TABLE OF CONTENTS

COPYRIGHT --2

INTRODUCTION   6

WHY SQL IS ESSENTIAL IN THE MODERN WORLD   6

CHAPTER 1: CHAPTER 1: INTRODUCTION TO SQL AND DATABASES   14

CHAPTER 2: SETTING UP YOUR SQL ENVIRONMENT   21

CHAPTER 3: BASIC QUERIES – SELECT AND FROM   30

CHAPTER 4: FILTERING DATA WITH WHERE   38

CHAPTER 5: ORGANIZING RESULTS WITH ORDER BY AND GROUP BY   47

CHAPTER 6: JOINING TABLES FOR COMPLETE DATA VIEWS   56

CHAPTER 7: AGGREGATING DATA WITH COUNT, SUM, AVG, MIN, MAX   66

CHAPTER 8: INSERTING, UPDATING, AND DELETING DATA   76

CHAPTER 9: SUB QUERIES AND NESTED QUERIES   86

CHAPTER 10: ADVANCED FILTERING WITH LIKE, IN, BETWEEN, AND NULL HANDLING   95

CHAPTER 11: WORKING WITH DATES AND TIMES   105

CHAPTER 12: CREATING AND USING VIEWS   114

CHAPTER 13: STORED PROCEDURES AND FUNCTIONS   124

CHAPTER 14: TRANSACTIONS AND DATA INTEGRITY   134

CHAPTER 15: INDEXING FOR PERFORMANCE OPTIMIZATION   142

CHAPTER 16: DATABASE NORMALIZATION AND OPTIMIZATION TECHNIQUES   152

CHAPTER 17: WORKING WITH NON-RELATIONAL DATA IN SQL   162

CHAPTER 18: SECURITY AND PERMISSIONS   170

CHAPTER 19: BACKUP, RECOVERY, AND DATA MIGRATION
179

CHAPTER 20: SQL IN THE REAL WORLD – BEST PRACTICES AND TIPS
188

SQL MASTERY: A COMPREHENSIVE SUMMARY   196

INTRODUCTION

Why SQL Is Essential in the Modern World

In a digital era where data is both abundant and essential, knowing how to manage, query, and analyze data has become a vital skill. Whether you're an aspiring data analyst, an experienced software engineer, or a small business owner, SQL—Structured Query Language—serves as the gateway to unlocking powerful insights. This book, ***Practical SQL: Mastering Database Queries and Management***, is designed to be your comprehensive, jargon-free guide to understanding SQL and transforming data into actionable knowledge.

Section 1: The Power of Data and Why SQL Matters

Data is at the heart of virtually every modern organization. From tech giants to local businesses, everyone relies on data to make informed decisions, streamline operations, and even develop new products. With so much data available, the challenge isn't gathering information but organizing and extracting meaningful insights from it. That's where SQL comes in.

SQL isn't just another tool—it's the universal language of data. Originally developed in the 1970s, SQL has grown alongside the evolution of databases, adapting to new technological advances while remaining consistent in its foundational purpose: to help people interact with and manage data in relational databases. Understanding SQL gives you direct access to vast data stores and the ability to transform raw data into usable knowledge. With SQL, you can:

- Answer questions about customer behavior, product performance, and trends.
- Automate repetitive data tasks, like updating inventory or generating sales reports.
- Perform advanced data analysis by combining tables, filtering data, and creating custom queries.

Real-world applications of SQL range from managing simple customer contact lists to performing complex data analysis for business intelligence. This book is designed to empower you to make SQL work for your specific needs, offering practical, hands-on examples at every step.

Section 2: Who This Book Is For and What You'll Gain

This book is crafted for readers at all levels—from beginners who may have no prior experience with SQL to intermediate users who want to deepen their understanding and become confident in advanced database management techniques. By the end of this book, you will:

1. **Master the Core Concepts of SQL:** We'll start with foundational queries, filtering data, and organizing it into meaningful formats.

2. **Perform Advanced Data Manipulation:** Beyond basic queries, you'll learn techniques for handling large datasets, managing complex joins, and using advanced filtering methods.

3. **Manage Databases Effectively:** You'll not only learn how to retrieve data but also how to insert, update, and delete records, keeping your database both accurate and efficient.

4. **Optimize Performance for Real-World Applications:** In the later chapters, you'll explore how to optimize your queries and manage indexes for faster performance.

5. **Learn Data Security and Best Practices:** Understanding how to secure your database and control access is just as important as learning how to query it.

Throughout the book, each concept will be explained through real-world examples. By the end, you'll have the skills to handle common data challenges in any organization, whether you're querying a customer database, analyzing sales, or setting up an inventory system.

Section 3: SQL in the Real World - Realistic Examples of Its Impact

To make the concepts in this book accessible and relevant, we'll explore SQL through practical, everyday scenarios. Here are a few real-world examples that reflect the kinds of problems you'll learn to solve with SQL:

- **Example 1: Business Analytics for Decision Making** A small retail business wants to understand which products are performing well and which aren't. Using SQL, they can pull reports from their sales database to analyze trends over time, seasonal fluctuations, and customer preferences. This allows them to adjust inventory, focus on popular items, and identify underperforming products.

- **Example 2: E-Commerce Order Tracking** In e-commerce, keeping track of order statuses, delivery timelines, and customer feedback is critical. SQL enables e-commerce businesses to store, manage, and retrieve customer orders easily, providing timely updates for customers and creating reports to improve the overall order management process.

- **Example 3: Financial Analysis in Accounting** Accountants and financial analysts rely on SQL to handle large datasets in payroll, expenses, and revenue. With SQL, they can create reports on monthly spending, detect discrepancies, and even automate routine calculations, making it easier to maintain accurate financial records.

SQL's real-world impact reaches across industries—marketing, healthcare, logistics, education, and finance all rely on it for data-driven insights.

Section 4: Core Themes and Teaching Philosophy of This Book

The goal of ***Practical SQL*** is to make SQL approachable, empowering, and applicable. Here are a few core themes you'll notice throughout:

- **Practicality Over Theory:** SQL can sometimes be presented as highly technical or abstract. This book, however, emphasizes practicality by focusing on applications and examples you're likely to encounter in real-world scenarios.
- **Building Skills Incrementally:** Each chapter builds on the last, starting with the basics and moving towards advanced techniques. By following the book sequentially, you'll develop a solid foundation and steadily gain confidence in SQL.
- **Interactive Exercises and Real-World Projects:** Theory alone isn't enough. Each chapter includes exercises and example projects that challenge you to apply what you've learned, ensuring that you retain the skills and can adapt them to new situations.

This approach makes SQL not just accessible but also engaging, empowering you to apply it in your professional and personal projects.

Section 5: Overcoming Common Misconceptions About SQL

One common misconception about SQL is that it's only useful for data analysts or database administrators. In reality, SQL is a valuable tool for anyone who works with data. Whether you're in marketing, customer service, or management, the ability to access and interpret data quickly can help you make better decisions.

Another common myth is that SQL is difficult to learn. While the syntax can seem intimidating at first, SQL is highly logical and straightforward. Each command performs a specific task, making it easy to understand the purpose behind each statement. This book's step-by-step approach aims to help you build confidence with SQL, demystifying it along the way.

Section 6: What You'll Need to Get Started

One of the great things about SQL is that it doesn't require specialized or expensive software to learn. This book will guide you in setting up a free SQL environment (using tools like MySQL, PostgreSQL, or SQLite) so that you can experiment with queries, create tables, and manipulate data as you progress. All you need is a computer and the willingness to dive into hands-on learning.

Section 7: Chapter-by-Chapter Overview of What You'll Learn

To give you a clear picture of what's ahead, here's a preview of the book's key topics:

- **Chapter 1:** You'll get an introduction to SQL and understand the role of databases in storing and managing data.

- **Chapter 2 to Chapter 5:** We'll cover the essential SQL commands: SELECT, WHERE, ORDER BY, and GROUP BY. These chapters will equip you with skills to filter, sort, and group data effectively.

- **Chapter 6 to Chapter 8:** You'll learn how to join tables, manipulate data with INSERT, UPDATE, and DELETE, and start working with subqueries to solve complex problems.

- **Chapter 9 to Chapter 12:** As you advance, you'll explore topics like pattern matching with LIKE, handling NULL values, working with dates and times, and creating views.

- **Chapter 13 to Chapter 15:** These chapters introduce you to stored procedures, indexing, and query optimization techniques—crucial skills for improving performance and efficiency.

- **Chapter 16 to Chapter 18:** Here, we'll cover database normalization, working with non-relational data, and essential security practices to ensure data integrity.

- **Chapter 19 to Chapter 20:** You'll wrap up by learning about database backups, migrations, and best practices for SQL in professional settings.

Each chapter provides not only a deep dive into a specific topic but also practical exercises and projects that help cement your knowledge and experience.

Section 8: Final Words – Your Journey to SQL Mastery

Practical SQL is more than just a technical manual—it's a guide to using SQL as a real-world tool to answer questions, solve problems, and drive informed decision-making. By the end of this book, you'll have not only a working knowledge of SQL syntax but also the confidence to tackle data challenges on your own.

Ready to begin your journey? Turn the page, and let's get started with SQL.

CHAPTER 1: CHAPTER 1: INTRODUCTION TO SQL AND DATABASES

Welcome to *Practical SQL*! In this first chapter, we'll lay the groundwork for everything you'll be learning about SQL and relational databases. You'll gain a clear understanding of what SQL is, why it's so powerful, and how relational databases are designed to organize and manage data. We'll use a simple, real-world example of tracking sales data for a small business to illustrate core SQL concepts in a relatable, practical way.

Section 1.1: What is SQL?

SQL, or **Structured Query Language**, is the standard language used to communicate with relational databases. It allows you to interact with data by writing queries—structured commands that perform specific actions. SQL helps users retrieve, insert, update, and delete data within a database, making it incredibly versatile for data management and analysis.

SQL is highly readable and structured, so each command has a specific purpose and format, making it approachable even if you're new to coding or database management.

Section 1.2: What is a Relational Database?

A **relational database** is a digital system designed to store data in a structured, organized way. This data is saved in tables—much like a spreadsheet—with rows and columns. Each table in a relational

14

database contains related information about a specific topic, and tables can be connected to one another through unique identifiers called keys. This relationship between tables gives relational databases their name and allows for complex, multi-table queries that produce highly useful insights.

For example, imagine a small business, such as a local coffee shop, that wants to track sales data, customer orders, and inventory. Instead of keeping all this information in separate files, a relational database allows the coffee shop to store and link these types of information in a unified system. This setup enables the shop to see, for example, which customers bought which items, or which items are running low in stock.

Section 1.3: Real-World Application – Tracking Sales Data for a Small Business

To understand the value of SQL, let's consider how it might be used to manage sales data for a small business, like our coffee shop example. Imagine the business owner wants to answer questions like:

- Which products are the best sellers?
- What are the total sales per day or per month?
- Who are the most frequent customers?

A relational database can store all this data and allow for easy access to answer these questions.

Here's how we might organize this information in tables:

1. **Customers Table**: Contains information about each customer, such as their name, contact details, and any customer loyalty data.

2. **Orders Table**: Stores details of each sale, including the date of sale, the customer who made the purchase, and the items purchased.

3. **Products Table**: Holds data on each product, including product name, price, and inventory levels.

4. **Order_Items Table**: Links each order to the specific products included, tracking quantity and individual item details.

Using these tables, SQL queries can quickly provide insights by connecting and extracting data across them. For example, a simple SQL query can list all orders placed by a specific customer, calculate total sales for a given month, or identify the most popular products over time.

Section 1.4: Essential SQL Concepts – Tables, Records, and Fields

To work with SQL and relational databases effectively, it's essential to understand three basic elements: **tables, records (rows), and fields (columns)**.

1. **Tables**: In SQL, a **table** is a collection of data organized in a grid format of rows and columns, like a spreadsheet. Each table is usually focused on a single subject, such as "Customers" or "Products."

- o **Example**: The *Customers* table might contain columns for Customer ID, Name, Email, and Phone Number.

2. **Records (Rows)**: Each row, or **record**, in a table represents a single item or entry in that table. For instance, a record in the *Customers* table would contain all the details for one customer. Every row in a table should have a unique identifier called a **primary key**.

   - o **Example**: If we have three customers, there would be three rows in the *Customers* table, each row containing details for one customer.

3. **Fields (Columns)**: Each column, or **field**, in a table represents a specific attribute of the data in that table. For example, in the *Products* table, we could have fields like Product Name, Price, and Stock Level. Each field applies to every record in the table.

   - o **Example**: The *Products* table may have fields like Product ID, Name, Price, and Stock Level. Each product listed in the table will have these details recorded in separate columns.

Understanding these basic elements is crucial as they form the foundation for everything you'll be doing in SQL. Every SQL query you write will interact with tables, records, and fields in some way, whether it's filtering data, combining tables, or updating records.

Section 1.5: Basic SQL Query Structure

The structure of an SQL query is consistent and straightforward, making it easy to understand even for beginners. The most basic SQL query consists of the following parts:

1. **SELECT**: This is used to specify which fields (columns) you want to retrieve data from.
2. **FROM**: Indicates the table where the data resides.
3. **WHERE**: (Optional) This allows you to filter data based on specific conditions.

Let's consider a simple query to retrieve data from a *Products* table to see which items have fewer than 10 units in stock.

sql

Copy code

```
SELECT ProductName, StockLevel
FROM Products
WHERE StockLevel < 10;
```

In this query:

- SELECT ProductName, StockLevel: Specifies that we want the Product Name and Stock Level columns.
- FROM Products: Indicates that we're retrieving data from the *Products* table.
- WHERE StockLevel < 10: Filters the results to only show products with a stock level of fewer than 10 units.

The result is a list of products that need restocking, a quick insight that could directly benefit our coffee shop owner.

Section 1.6: Common SQL Data Types

In SQL, each field (column) has a **data type**. Data types define the kind of data that can be stored in a particular field, which helps maintain data integrity. Here are some of the most common data types:

- **INT**: For integers (whole numbers).
- **VARCHAR**: For variable-length strings, often used for text.
- **DATE**: For storing date values.
- **FLOAT**: For numbers with decimal places.
- **BOOLEAN**: For true/false values.

For example, in our *Products* table, we might use:

- ProductID (INT): A unique identifier for each product.
- ProductName (VARCHAR): The name of each product.
- Price (FLOAT): The price of each product.
- StockLevel (INT): The number of units available in stock.

Each of these data types helps structure the information so the database can process it efficiently and consistently.

Section 1.7: Key Takeaways and Preparing for the Next Chapter

This chapter introduced you to the basics of SQL and relational databases, using a small business example to show how SQL can solve real-world problems by organizing and managing data. You've learned about tables, records, fields, and the essential structure of SQL queries.

In the next chapter, we'll dive into setting up your SQL environment and creating your first database. You'll get hands-on experience with creating tables, defining fields, and inputting sample data, preparing you to start building and querying your own databases.

By keeping things practical, we'll build on this foundation in each chapter, guiding you from beginner SQL concepts to advanced query techniques and data management practices. Let's move on to Chapter 2 and start setting up your first database!

CHAPTER 2: SETTING UP YOUR SQL ENVIRONMENT

Welcome to Chapter 2! Now that you understand the basics of SQL and relational databases, it's time to set up your own SQL environment. By the end of this chapter, you'll have everything you need to start practicing SQL commands, including a database you can query and manage. We'll walk through the installation and setup of popular SQL databases, compare SQL interfaces, and provide a hands-on exercise to create your first database and tables.

Section 2.1: Choosing the Right SQL Database for Your Needs

There are many SQL database systems available, but three of the most popular (and beginner-friendly) ones are **MySQL**, **PostgreSQL**, and **SQLite**. Here's a brief overview to help you choose the best one for your setup:

1. **MySQL**: One of the most widely used SQL databases, especially popular in web applications and known for its speed and reliability. MySQL is open-source and is a great choice for beginners, offering a good balance between simplicity and functionality.

2. **PostgreSQL**: Another powerful, open-source SQL database known for its advanced features and standards compliance. PostgreSQL is often chosen for applications that require

complex queries or strict data integrity and supports a wider range of data types and functions.

3. **SQLite**: A lightweight, self-contained SQL database that doesn't require a server installation. SQLite is ideal for quick setup, learning, and smaller applications. Many developers use SQLite for local projects or applications that don't require a heavy-duty database.

For this chapter, we'll walk through setting up each of these databases so you can choose the one that best fits your needs.

Section 2.2: Installing and Setting Up SQL Databases

Step 1: Installing MySQL

1. **Download MySQL**: Visit the MySQL official website and download the installer that matches your operating system (Windows, MacOS, or Linux).

2. **Run the Installer**: Follow the installation instructions provided. You may be prompted to set a root password, which is an essential security measure.

3. **Choose Configuration Options**: During setup, you can select options such as the default character set and whether you want MySQL to run automatically as a service. It's generally safe to use the default settings if you're unsure.

4. **Open MySQL**: After installation, open MySQL Workbench (a GUI tool for MySQL), or access MySQL via the

command-line interface (CLI) to start issuing SQL commands.

Step 2: Installing PostgreSQL

1. **Download PostgreSQL**: Visit the PostgreSQL website and select the installer for your operating system.
2. **Run the Installer**: During the setup, PostgreSQL will prompt you to set a password for the database superuser (postgres). Be sure to remember this password, as you'll need it for database access.
3. **Install pgAdmin (Optional)**: pgAdmin is a popular GUI tool that comes with PostgreSQL, allowing you to manage your database in a user-friendly way.
4. **Launch PostgreSQL**: Open pgAdmin or use the PostgreSQL CLI to start working with your new database.

Step 3: Setting Up SQLite

1. **Download SQLite**: Head to the SQLite website and download the precompiled binaries for your operating system.
2. **Extract and Place SQLite in a Convenient Location**: Extract the files and place the SQLite executable in a folder that's easy to access.

3. **Launch SQLite**: Open your command line, navigate to the directory containing the SQLite executable, and type sqlite3 to start the SQLite environment.

4. **No Additional Setup Required**: SQLite is ready to go immediately—no server setup or GUI tools required (though you can download GUI tools like DB Browser for SQLite if you prefer).

Section 2.3: Exploring SQL Interfaces – CLI vs. GUI Tools

Once your SQL database is set up, you'll need an interface to interact with it. There are two main types:

1. **Command-Line Interface (CLI)**: The CLI is a text-based interface that allows you to enter SQL commands directly. It's lightweight and fast but requires familiarity with command syntax. The CLI can be accessed in MySQL, PostgreSQL, and SQLite, and it's great for those who prefer working directly with code.

   o **Benefits**: Lightweight, less resource-intensive, and available on almost any system.

   o **Drawbacks**: No visual aids or drag-and-drop options, which can make navigation more challenging for beginners.

2. **Graphical User Interface (GUI) Tools**: GUI tools, such as MySQL Workbench, pgAdmin, and DB Browser for SQLite, provide a user-friendly interface with features like visual

table editors, drag-and-drop query builders, and data visualization options.

- o **Benefits**: Easier for beginners, especially for viewing data structures and working with complex databases.
- o **Drawbacks**: May require more system resources and can feel slower than the CLI for some tasks.

In this chapter, you'll practice with both the CLI and GUI tools to get a feel for their different advantages. Try both options to see which interface best suits your style.

Section 2.4: Hands-On Practice – Creating Your First Database and Tables

Now that your SQL environment is set up, let's create your first database and tables. This exercise will help you become familiar with the commands and structures of SQL.

Step 1: Creating a Database

1. **Open Your SQL Interface** (CLI or GUI).
2. **Run a Command to Create the Database**:
   - o **MySQL/PostgreSQL**: In the command prompt or GUI, type the following command to create a database named ShopDB:

   sql

Copy code

```
CREATE DATABASE ShopDB;
```

- o **SQLite**: Since SQLite doesn't use the CREATE DATABASE command, open SQLite and specify a new database file:

bash

Copy code

```
sqlite3 ShopDB.db
```

3. **Switch to the New Database**:
   - o **MySQL/PostgreSQL**:

sql

Copy code

```
USE ShopDB;
```

   - o **SQLite**: You are already working in ShopDB.db.

This new database, ShopDB, will serve as our sandbox environment for all future exercises and examples.

Step 2: Creating Your First Table – Customers

Next, let's create a simple table called Customers to store data about the shop's customers.

1. **Enter the Command to Create the Table**:

sql

Copy code

```
CREATE TABLE Customers (
    CustomerID INT PRIMARY KEY,
    Name VARCHAR(50),
    Email VARCHAR(50),
    Phone VARCHAR(15)
);
```

Here's what each part of this command does:

- CREATE TABLE Customers: Tells SQL to create a new table named Customers.
- CustomerID INT PRIMARY KEY: Creates a unique identifier for each customer. The **PRIMARY KEY** constraint ensures that each value in the CustomerID column is unique.
- Name VARCHAR(50): Creates a field for the customer's name, allowing up to 50 characters.
- Email VARCHAR(50): Creates a field for the customer's email address, with a limit of 50 characters.
- Phone VARCHAR(15): Creates a field for the customer's phone number, allowing up to 15 characters.

2. **Verify the Table Creation**:

o   To check if your table was created successfully, use a command to list all tables in the database:

sql

Copy code

SHOW TABLES; -- MySQL

\dt   -- PostgreSQL

.tables   -- SQLite

Step 3: Adding Data to the Customers Table

Now let's add a few records to the Customers table.

1. **Insert Sample Data**:

sql

Copy code

INSERT INTO Customers (CustomerID, Name, Email, Phone)

VALUES (1, 'John Doe', 'john@example.com', '555-1234');

INSERT INTO Customers (CustomerID, Name, Email, Phone)

VALUES (2, 'Jane Smith', 'jane@example.com', '555-5678');

Here, we're using the INSERT INTO command to add a new row (record) into the Customers table.

2. **Check the Data**:

  o Retrieve the data you entered to ensure it was saved correctly:

  sql

  Copy code

  SELECT * FROM Customers;

3. This command will display all the records in the Customers table.

Section 2.5: Summary and What's Next

Congratulations! You've set up your SQL environment, explored different SQL interfaces, and created your first database and table. You now have a foundation to build on as you begin learning about querying, managing, and analyzing data in SQL.

In the next chapter, we'll dive deeper into SQL queries, focusing on retrieving data from tables using the essential SELECT and FROM commands. These foundational skills will help you start answering questions and gaining insights from your data.

Let's keep moving toward mastering SQL!

CHAPTER 3: BASIC QUERIES – SELECT AND FROM

Welcome to Chapter 3! In this chapter, you'll learn about two of the most fundamental SQL commands, SELECT and FROM. These commands allow you to retrieve data from tables within a database, making them the foundation of almost every SQL query. By the end of this chapter, you'll understand how to use SELECT and FROM to perform basic data retrieval tasks, and you'll complete some practical exercises to reinforce these concepts.

Section 3.1: Understanding the SELECT Command

The SELECT command is used to specify which columns of data you want to retrieve from a table. Think of it as a tool that lets you "select" specific pieces of information to view.

The basic structure of a SELECT statement is as follows:

sql

Copy code

SELECT column1, column2, ...

FROM table_name;

Here's what each part does:

- SELECT: Tells SQL to retrieve data from a table.

- column1, column2, ...: Specifies the columns (fields) you want to retrieve. You can select one column, multiple columns, or all columns.
- FROM table_name: Identifies the table where the data resides.

Example: If you have a table called Customers and you want to view the Name and Email columns, you would write:

sql

Copy code

SELECT Name, Email

FROM Customers;

This command will return only the Name and Email columns from the Customers table.

Section 3.2: The FROM Command

The FROM command is used to specify which table you're pulling data from. You'll always use FROM in conjunction with SELECT, as it tells SQL where to find the data to retrieve.

For instance, let's say you want to see all columns in the Customers table. You can use the wildcard *, which represents "all columns." Here's how you would write that query:

sql

Copy code

SELECT *

FROM Customers;

This query retrieves every column and every row in the Customers table. It's useful when you want to view all data but can lead to large query results, so it's best used selectively.

Section 3.3: Real-World Example – Retrieving Customer Lists from a Company Database

Let's apply what we've learned to a real-world scenario. Imagine you work at a company that wants to retrieve customer lists for marketing purposes. The database includes a Customers table with information like CustomerID, Name, Email, and Phone. Here are a few tasks you might encounter and the SQL queries you could use to solve them:

Task 1: Retrieve All Customer Names

To get a simple list of all customer names:

```sql
Copy code
SELECT Name
FROM Customers;
```

This query pulls just the Name column from the Customers table, which can be useful if you're preparing a list of customers for personalized email outreach.

Task 2: Retrieve Names and Email Addresses

Suppose the marketing team wants to reach out to customers via email. They request both the names and email addresses of all customers:

sql

Copy code

SELECT Name, Email

FROM Customers;

This query retrieves only the Name and Email columns, creating a more focused list for the email marketing team.

Task 3: Retrieve All Customer Data

If the team needs all available customer details for a comprehensive review, you would use:

sql

Copy code

SELECT *

FROM Customers;

This query returns all columns and rows in the Customers table, providing a complete view of customer information.

Each of these examples demonstrates how SELECT and FROM let you control what data you're retrieving based on specific needs.

Section 3.4: Practical Exercises to Reinforce Concepts

Now, let's try some hands-on exercises to solidify your understanding of the SELECT and FROM commands.

Exercise 1: Basic Column Selection

1. **Goal**: Retrieve the names of all customers from the Customers table.
2. **Expected Output**: A list of customer names.
3. **Solution**:

```sql
SELECT Name
FROM Customers;
```

Exercise 2: Multiple Column Selection

1. **Goal**: Retrieve both the names and email addresses of all customers.
2. **Expected Output**: A list showing customer names and their associated email addresses.
3. **Solution**:

```sql
SELECT Name, Email
FROM Customers;
```

Exercise 3: Select All Columns

1. **Goal**: Retrieve all columns in the Customers table.
2. **Expected Output**: The full details of every customer in the table.

3. **Solution**:

sql
SELECT *
FROM Customers;

Exercise 4: Exploring a Different Table

1. **Goal**: Assume you have a second table named Orders with columns OrderID, CustomerID, OrderDate, and Amount. Retrieve only the OrderDate and Amount columns.
2. **Expected Output**: A list of order dates and amounts.
3. **Solution**:

sql
SELECT OrderDate, Amount
FROM Orders;

These exercises cover the most common ways to use SELECT and FROM. Practice them on your own database to get comfortable with retrieving data in various formats.

Section 3.5: Common Mistakes and Best Practices

While working with SELECT and FROM, it's easy to make some common mistakes. Here are a few tips and best practices:

1. **Always Specify the Table in the FROM Clause**: Forgetting to include the FROM clause will result in an error, as SQL won't know where to retrieve the data from.

2. **Use Wildcards (*) Sparingly**: While SELECT * is useful, it can return a large amount of data, which may slow down queries in large databases. Use it only when you truly need every column.

3. **Specify Columns Explicitly**: Specifying individual columns instead of using * makes your queries faster and your intentions clearer, which is especially useful in collaborative environments.

4. **Practice Writing Queries Consistently**: SQL is not case-sensitive, so select, SELECT, and SeLeCt are all technically correct. However, it's good practice to write SQL keywords in uppercase (e.g., SELECT, FROM) and table and column names in lowercase, as this makes the code easier to read and more standardized.

5. **Check Your Results**: Always review the output to ensure the query retrieves exactly what you expect. This helps catch potential issues early on.

Section 3.6: Summary and What's Next

In this chapter, you've learned the basics of the SELECT and FROM commands and how to retrieve data from tables. You've also completed practical exercises to practice selecting specific columns, multiple columns, and all columns in a table. With these skills, you can now start retrieving essential data from your database.

In the next chapter, we'll introduce the WHERE clause, which allows you to filter data based on specific conditions. This will give you more control over the data you retrieve, helping you answer targeted questions and refine your queries.

Ready to take your SQL skills to the next level? Let's continue on to Chapter 4!

CHAPTER 4: FILTERING DATA WITH WHERE

In this chapter, we'll focus on one of the most powerful tools in SQL: the WHERE clause. The WHERE clause lets you filter data based on specific conditions, allowing you to retrieve only the rows that meet your criteria. By the end of this chapter, you'll understand how to use WHERE to narrow down data, apply simple conditions, and work with operators for more flexible filtering.

Section 4.1: Understanding the WHERE Clause

The WHERE clause is used to specify conditions that filter rows in a table. When you add a WHERE clause to a query, SQL will retrieve only the rows that satisfy the condition(s) you define. This makes WHERE essential for answering targeted questions or narrowing down results.

The structure of a WHERE clause looks like this:

sql
Copy code
```
SELECT column1, column2, ...
FROM table_name
WHERE condition;
```

- **SELECT**: Identifies the columns to retrieve.
- **FROM**: Identifies the table to retrieve data from.

- **WHERE**: Specifies the condition(s) that rows must meet to be included in the result.

For example, if you have a Customers table and want to retrieve customers based in New York, you could use:

sql
Copy code
SELECT Name, Email
FROM Customers
WHERE City = 'New York';

In this example, SQL retrieves only the rows where the City column has the value 'New York'.

Section 4.2: Real-World Application – Narrowing Down Customers Based on Location or Purchase History

Let's apply the WHERE clause to some practical scenarios. Imagine a retail company that wants to focus its marketing efforts on specific customer segments based on location or purchase history. Here are a few real-world tasks and corresponding SQL queries:

Task 1: Retrieve Customers from a Specific Location

The company wants to contact only customers based in California for a regional promotion. Assuming the Customers table includes columns for CustomerID, Name, and State, the SQL query would look like this:

sql

SELECT CustomerID, Name

FROM Customers

WHERE State = 'California';

This query retrieves only the customers who live in California, allowing the marketing team to target their outreach more effectively.

Task 2: Find Customers Who Made Purchases Above a Certain Amount

If the company wants to focus on high-spending customers, it could look for customers who have spent over $500 in total. Assuming there's an Orders table with columns CustomerID, OrderID, and Amount, we can query it as follows:

sql

SELECT CustomerID, OrderID, Amount

FROM Orders

WHERE Amount > 500;

This query retrieves all orders where the amount is greater than $500. You could refine this further by joining it with the Customers table to get more information about each customer.

Task 3: Retrieve Customers Who Made Purchases in the Past Month

Suppose the company wants to reach out to customers who have made a recent purchase. Assuming the Orders table includes a column OrderDate, you can use the following query to retrieve orders from the past month:

sql

SELECT CustomerID, OrderID, OrderDate

FROM Orders

WHERE OrderDate >= '2023-09-01' AND OrderDate <= '2023-09-30';

This query uses a date range to filter records, retrieving only orders placed between September 1 and September 30, 2023.

Section 4.3: Using Simple Conditions and Operators

The WHERE clause supports various conditions and operators to help you refine your queries. Here's an overview of the most commonly used operators:

1. **Equality (=)**: Finds exact matches.
   - Example: WHERE State = 'California'
2. **Inequality (<> or !=)**: Finds records that don't match a specific value.
   - Example: WHERE City <> 'New York'
3. **Greater Than / Less Than (>, <)**: Compares numerical or date values.
   - Example: WHERE Amount > 500
4. **Greater Than or Equal To / Less Than or Equal To (>=, <=)**: Allows for inclusive range comparisons.

   o   Example: WHERE OrderDate >= '2023-09-01'

5. **AND / OR**: Combines multiple conditions.

   o   Example: WHERE State = 'California' AND Amount
       > 500

6. **IN**: Allows filtering based on a list of possible values.

   o   Example: WHERE State IN ('California', 'New York',
       'Texas')

7. **BETWEEN**: Finds values within a specified range (often
   used for dates or numbers).

   o   Example: WHERE Amount BETWEEN 100 AND
       500

8. **LIKE**: Finds patterns in text (we'll explore this in more
   depth in Chapter 10).

   o   Example: WHERE Name LIKE 'J%' (finds names
       that start with "J")

Section 4.4: Practice Queries with WHERE Clause

Let's try some practice queries to reinforce your understanding of
WHERE and different operators.

Exercise 1: Retrieve Customers from a Specific State

1. **Goal**: Retrieve customers from New York.

2. **Expected Output**: A list of customers whose State is New
   York.

3. **Solution**:

```sql
sql
SELECT CustomerID, Name
FROM Customers
WHERE State = 'New York';
```

Exercise 2: Find High-Value Orders

1. **Goal**: Retrieve all orders where the amount is greater than $300.
2. **Expected Output**: A list of order IDs and amounts greater than $300.
3. **Solution**:

```sql
sql
SELECT OrderID, Amount
FROM Orders
WHERE Amount > 300;
```

Exercise 3: Retrieve Customers Who Are Not in California

1. **Goal**: Retrieve customers who do not reside in California.
2. **Expected Output**: A list of customers in states other than California.
3. **Solution**:

```sql
sql
SELECT CustomerID, Name, State
```

FROM Customers

WHERE State <> 'California';

Exercise 4: Using AND to Combine Conditions

1. **Goal**: Retrieve all orders over $300 that were placed in September 2023.
2. **Expected Output**: A list of orders with amounts greater than $300 and order dates within the specified date range.
3. **Solution**:

sql

```
SELECT OrderID, CustomerID, Amount, OrderDate
FROM Orders
WHERE Amount > 300 AND OrderDate BETWEEN '2023-09-01' AND '2023-09-30';
```

Exercise 5: Filter Based on a List of Values Using IN

1. **Goal**: Retrieve customers who live in California, Texas, or New York.
2. **Expected Output**: A list of customers from the three specified states.
3. **Solution**:

sql

```
SELECT CustomerID, Name, State
```

FROM Customers

WHERE State IN ('California', 'Texas', 'New York');

Section 4.5: Common Mistakes and Best Practices with WHERE Clause

When using WHERE, keep these tips in mind to avoid common mistakes:

1. **Check for Typographical Errors**: Typos in column names or values can lead to unexpected results or errors. Double-check your syntax, especially with strings in quotes.

2. **Order Matters with AND/OR**: When combining conditions, be cautious with AND and OR operators. Use parentheses to ensure conditions are evaluated as intended, particularly in complex queries.

   o Example: WHERE (State = 'California' OR State = 'New York') AND Amount > 500

3. **Use BETWEEN and IN for Readability**: For ranges and lists, BETWEEN and IN are more readable and can help prevent mistakes compared to using multiple AND/OR conditions.

4. **Test with Sample Queries**: It's good practice to test parts of a query before combining them into a larger query, especially when multiple conditions are involved.

Section 4.6: Summary and What's Next

In this chapter, you learned how to use the WHERE clause to filter data based on specific conditions. You explored various operators, including =, >, <, AND, OR, IN, and BETWEEN, and completed practice exercises to build your understanding of filtering in SQL.

The WHERE clause is a versatile tool that enables targeted data retrieval, making it invaluable for real-world applications like segmenting customers or analyzing purchase trends. In the next chapter, we'll expand on this by learning how to sort and group data with the ORDER BY and GROUP BY commands, giving you even more control over your query results.

CHAPTER 5: ORGANIZING RESULTS WITH ORDER BY AND GROUP BY

Welcome to Chapter 5! In this chapter, we'll cover two essential SQL commands for organizing and summarizing query results: ORDER BY and GROUP BY. By learning to sort and group data, you'll be able to create organized and meaningful reports, such as monthly sales summaries or rankings based on sales volume. By the end of this chapter, you'll be able to apply these commands effectively to your queries and build more powerful insights.

Section 5.1: Sorting Data with ORDER BY

The ORDER BY clause allows you to sort data in ascending or descending order based on one or more columns. Sorting data is helpful for tasks like ranking top-performing products, identifying highest-spending customers, or reviewing recent orders.

The basic structure of the ORDER BY clause is:

sql
SELECT column1, column2, ...
FROM table_name
ORDER BY column1 [ASC|DESC], column2 [ASC|DESC], ...;

- **ORDER BY**: Specifies that the data should be sorted.
- **column1, column2, ...**: Lists the columns you want to sort by, in the order of priority.

- **ASC**: Sorts results in ascending order (default).
- **DESC**: Sorts results in descending order.

Example: Sorting customers by their names in alphabetical order.

sql
SELECT Name, Email
FROM Customers
ORDER BY Name ASC;

This query retrieves all customer names and email addresses, sorted alphabetically by the Name column. Using ASC here is optional since ascending order is the default.

Section 5.2: Sorting by Multiple Columns

You can also sort by multiple columns to add another level of organization. SQL will sort by the first column specified, and if there are duplicate values, it will then sort by the next column.

Example: Sorting orders by CustomerID first, and then by OrderDate in descending order to show the most recent orders first.

sql
SELECT CustomerID, OrderID, OrderDate, Amount
FROM Orders
ORDER BY CustomerID ASC, OrderDate DESC;

This query sorts orders first by CustomerID in ascending order and then by OrderDate in descending order for each customer. This type of sorting is useful when you want to view customers' most recent orders at the top of the list.

Section 5.3: Grouping Data with GROUP BY

The GROUP BY clause allows you to group rows that share the same values in specified columns, helping you summarize data. This is especially useful when combined with aggregate functions like SUM, COUNT, AVG, MIN, and MAX.

The basic structure of a GROUP BY query is:

sql

```
SELECT column1, aggregate_function(column2)
FROM table_name
GROUP BY column1;
```

- **GROUP BY**: Groups rows based on the values of the specified column(s).
- **aggregate_function**: A function that performs calculations on grouped data, like SUM or COUNT.

Example: Counting the number of orders for each customer.

sql

```
SELECT CustomerID, COUNT(OrderID) AS OrderCount
FROM Orders
GROUP BY CustomerID;
```

This query groups rows in the Orders table by CustomerID and uses COUNT to calculate the number of orders each customer has placed.

Section 5.4: Real-World Example – Generating Monthly Sales Summaries

Let's apply ORDER BY and GROUP BY in a practical example where we generate a monthly sales report. Imagine you work for a retail company that wants a report of total sales for each month. The Orders table has the following columns: OrderID, CustomerID, OrderDate, and Amount.

Step 1: Extracting the Month from the Order Date

To generate monthly summaries, we need to group orders by month. Assuming OrderDate is in YYYY-MM-DD format, you can extract the month and year from the date using the DATE_FORMAT function (in MySQL) or the EXTRACT function (in PostgreSQL). Here's an example in MySQL:

```sql
sql
SELECT DATE_FORMAT(OrderDate, '%Y-%m') AS Month,
SUM(Amount) AS TotalSales
FROM Orders
GROUP BY Month
ORDER BY Month ASC;
```

- DATE_FORMAT(OrderDate, '%Y-%m'): Extracts the year and month from the OrderDate.

- SUM(Amount): Calculates the total sales for each month.
- GROUP BY Month: Groups the data by each month.
- ORDER BY Month ASC: Sorts the results in chronological order.

Example Result:

Month   TotalSales

2023-01 5000

2023-02 4500

2023-03 6200

Step 2: Including More Details in the Summary

If you wanted a more detailed summary, you could include the count of orders per month alongside total sales:

sql

```sql
SELECT DATE_FORMAT(OrderDate, '%Y-%m') AS Month,
    COUNT(OrderID) AS OrderCount,
    SUM(Amount) AS TotalSales
FROM Orders
GROUP BY Month
ORDER BY Month ASC;
```

This query provides a more comprehensive monthly sales report by adding the number of orders placed in each month.

Section 5.5: Practice Queries with ORDER BY and GROUP BY

Now, let's try some practice queries to get comfortable with ORDER BY and GROUP BY.

Exercise 1: Sorting by Total Sales

1. **Goal**: Retrieve a list of customers, sorted by total sales in descending order.
2. **Expected Output**: A list of customers, showing the highest-spending customers at the top.
3. **Solution**:

```sql
SELECT CustomerID, SUM(Amount) AS TotalSpent
FROM Orders
GROUP BY CustomerID
ORDER BY TotalSpent DESC;
```

Exercise 2: Monthly Sales Summary with Highest Sales First

1. **Goal**: Generate a monthly sales summary, sorted by total sales in descending order.
2. **Expected Output**: A report showing months with the highest sales at the top.
3. **Solution**:

sql

SELECT DATE_FORMAT(OrderDate, '%Y-%m') AS Month,

   SUM(Amount) AS TotalSales

FROM Orders

GROUP BY Month

ORDER BY TotalSales DESC;

Exercise 3: Count Orders by State (Advanced)

1. **Goal**: Retrieve a count of orders placed by customers in each state.

2. **Expected Output**: A list showing each state and the total number of orders from that state.

3. **Solution** (assuming Customers and Orders are linked by CustomerID):

sql

SELECT State, COUNT(OrderID) AS OrderCount

FROM Customers

JOIN Orders ON Customers.CustomerID = Orders.CustomerID

GROUP BY State

ORDER BY OrderCount DESC;

This query uses a JOIN to combine Customers and Orders, then groups by State to get a count of orders from each state.

Section 5.6: Common Mistakes and Best Practices with ORDER BY and GROUP BY

Here are some tips to avoid common mistakes when using ORDER BY and GROUP BY:

1. **Use Aggregate Functions with GROUP BY**: When using GROUP BY, make sure that any column not listed in the GROUP BY clause is used within an aggregate function (e.g., SUM, COUNT). Without this, SQL may produce an error or unexpected results.

2. **Ordering by Aggregate Results**: When sorting by aggregate results, use the column alias in the ORDER BY clause for clarity.
   - Example: ORDER BY TotalSales DESC rather than recalculating the aggregate.

3. **Consider Readability with Aliases**: Use aliases (e.g., AS TotalSales) to make query results and ORDER BY/GROUP BY clauses more readable. Aliases can make a query's purpose clear, especially in complex reports.

4. **Testing Grouping Results**: For complex GROUP BY queries, run initial tests without the ORDER BY clause. Verify the grouping logic first, then add sorting for the final output.

Section 5.7: Summary and What's Next

In this chapter, you learned how to organize query results using ORDER BY and summarize data with GROUP BY. You saw practical applications for generating reports, such as monthly sales summaries, and completed exercises to reinforce your understanding of these concepts.

Next, in Chapter 6, we'll move on to joining tables with SQL's various JOIN commands. This will allow you to combine data from multiple tables and create more comprehensive queries to answer complex questions about your data.

Keep up the great work—you're building a strong foundation for SQL master

Chapter 6: Joining Tables for Complete Data Views

Welcome to Chapter 6! This chapter focuses on one of the most powerful features of SQL: joining tables. By using JOIN commands, you can combine data from multiple tables, allowing you to create richer, more comprehensive queries. In this chapter, you'll learn about the different types of joins—INNER JOIN, LEFT JOIN, RIGHT JOIN, and FULL JOIN—and how they work. We'll apply these concepts in a real-world scenario to create sales reports by joining customer and order tables.

Section 6.1: Understanding Different JOIN Types

In relational databases, data is often split across multiple tables to avoid redundancy and maintain efficiency. For example, customer information might be in one table (Customers), while order details are in another (Orders). To generate complete data views, we need to join these tables. Here's an overview of the four main types of joins and their purposes:

1. **INNER JOIN**: Combines rows from two tables only where there's a match in both tables. If a record exists in one table but not the other, it won't appear in the result.

    o **Use Case**: Retrieve orders for customers who have made a purchase.

2. **LEFT JOIN** (or **LEFT OUTER JOIN**): Returns all rows from the left table, along with matching rows from the right table. If there's no match in the right table, it returns NULL for those columns.

   o **Use Case**: Retrieve all customers, including those who haven't placed any orders.

3. **RIGHT JOIN** (or **RIGHT OUTER JOIN**): Returns all rows from the right table and matching rows from the left table. If there's no match in the left table, it returns NULL for those columns.

   o **Use Case**: Retrieve all orders, including those where no customer information is available (e.g., anonymous or guest orders).

4. **FULL JOIN** (or **FULL OUTER JOIN**): Combines all rows from both tables, returning matching rows and including NULL for non-matching rows from both sides.

   o **Use Case**: Retrieve a complete list of customers and orders, showing NULL where there's no match on either side.

Section 6.2: Real-World Scenario – Joining Customer and Order Tables to Create Sales Reports

To see joins in action, let's consider a scenario where a retail business wants to generate sales reports that combine data from two tables:

- **Customers Table**: Stores customer information, including CustomerID, Name, and Email.
- **Orders Table**: Stores order details, including OrderID, CustomerID, OrderDate, and Amount.

In this scenario, each row in the Orders table has a CustomerID field that links it to the Customers table. We'll use joins to answer common business questions.

Example 1: Using INNER JOIN to Retrieve Orders for Customers

Suppose the business wants to retrieve information about all customers who have placed an order, including each order's amount and date. Using an INNER JOIN, we can combine rows from the Customers and Orders tables where CustomerID exists in both tables.

sql
Copy code

```
SELECT        Customers.CustomerID,        Customers.Name,
Orders.OrderID, Orders.OrderDate, Orders.Amount
FROM Customers
INNER    JOIN    Orders    ON    Customers.CustomerID    =
Orders.CustomerID;
```

- **INNER JOIN**: Combines rows only where CustomerID matches in both tables.

- **ON Customers.CustomerID = Orders.CustomerID**: Specifies the condition for the join.

This query returns only those customers who have made a purchase, excluding customers without orders.

Example 2: Using LEFT JOIN to Include All Customers, Even Those Without Orders

Now suppose the business wants a complete customer list, showing all customers, including those who haven't placed any orders. Using a LEFT JOIN ensures that all rows from the Customers table are included, even if there's no corresponding row in the Orders table. If a customer hasn't placed any orders, the OrderID, OrderDate, and Amount fields will appear as NULL.

sql

SELECT Customers.CustomerID, Customers.Name, Orders.OrderID, Orders.OrderDate, Orders.Amount

FROM Customers

LEFT JOIN Orders ON Customers.CustomerID = Orders.CustomerID;

This query is useful for finding customers who haven't made a purchase, which can be valuable for targeted marketing efforts.

Example 3: Using RIGHT JOIN to Retrieve All Orders, Even Those Without Customer Data

In cases where the business needs a report of all orders, including those that may not have corresponding customer data (such as guest orders), a RIGHT JOIN can be used. This ensures that all rows from the Orders table appear in the result, even if there's no match in the Customers table.

sql

```
SELECT          Customers.CustomerID,          Customers.Name,
Orders.OrderID, Orders.OrderDate, Orders.Amount
FROM Customers
RIGHT   JOIN   Orders   ON   Customers.CustomerID   =
Orders.CustomerID;
```

If an order doesn't have a matching CustomerID in the Customers table, the CustomerID and Name columns will be NULL in the result.

Example 4: Using FULL JOIN to Retrieve All Customers and All Orders

To create a comprehensive report that lists all customers and all orders, regardless of matches, use a FULL JOIN. This includes all rows from both tables, showing NULL where there's no match on either side.

sql

SELECT   Customers.CustomerID,   Customers.Name,
Orders.OrderID, Orders.OrderDate, Orders.Amount

FROM Customers

FULL   JOIN   Orders   ON   Customers.CustomerID   =
Orders.CustomerID;

This query is helpful if you need a complete view of all customers
and orders, including cases where there's missing data.

Section 6.3: Exercises to Practice Joining and Combining Tables

Now, let's put these join types to practice with some exercises.

Exercise 1: Find Orders for Each Customer

1. **Goal**: Retrieve a list of all customers who have placed an
   order, showing the order details for each.
2. **Expected Output**: A list with each customer's name,
   OrderID, OrderDate, and Amount.
3. **Solution**:

   sql

   SELECT   Customers.Name,   Orders.OrderID,
   Orders.OrderDate, Orders.Amount

   FROM Customers

   INNER   JOIN   Orders   ON   Customers.CustomerID   =
   Orders.CustomerID;

Exercise 2: Identify Customers Without Orders

1. **Goal**: Retrieve a list of all customers, including those who haven't placed any orders.

2. **Expected Output**: A list with each customer's name, and NULL in OrderID, OrderDate, and Amount for customers without orders.

3. **Solution**:

sql

SELECT Customers.Name, Orders.OrderID, Orders.OrderDate, Orders.Amount

FROM Customers

LEFT JOIN Orders ON Customers.CustomerID = Orders.CustomerID;

Exercise 3: Find All Orders and Their Customer Details

1. **Goal**: Retrieve a list of all orders, including orders that have no matching customer information.

2. **Expected Output**: A list of orders showing each OrderID, OrderDate, Amount, and customer details if available.

3. **Solution**:

sql

SELECT Customers.CustomerID, Customers.Name, Orders.OrderID, Orders.OrderDate, Orders.Amount

FROM Customers

RIGHT JOIN Orders ON Customers.CustomerID = Orders.CustomerID;

Exercise 4: Comprehensive List of All Customers and All Orders

1. **Goal**: Create a list showing all customers and all orders, even if they don't have matching entries.

2. **Expected Output**: A comprehensive list where each row shows CustomerID, Name, OrderID, OrderDate, and Amount, with NULL values for non-matching rows.

3. **Solution**:

sql

SELECT Customers.CustomerID, Customers.Name, Orders.OrderID, Orders.OrderDate, Orders.Amount

FROM Customers

FULL JOIN Orders ON Customers.CustomerID = Orders.CustomerID;

Section 6.4: Common Mistakes and Best Practices with Joins

Here are some tips to avoid common mistakes when working with joins:

1. **Verify Matching Columns**: Ensure you're joining tables on matching columns (e.g., CustomerID in both Customers and Orders). Joining on unrelated columns will produce incorrect results.

2. **Use the Correct Join Type**: Choose the join type based on the results you want:
   - Use INNER JOIN when you only need rows with matches in both tables.
   - Use LEFT JOIN when you want all rows from the left table, including unmatched rows.
   - Use RIGHT JOIN when you want all rows from the right table, including unmatched rows.
   - Use FULL JOIN when you need all rows from both tables.

3. **Check for NULLs**: In LEFT, RIGHT, and FULL JOIN results, you may get NULL values in unmatched columns. Plan your queries accordingly, especially if you need to handle or filter out NULL values.

4. **Optimize for Performance**: Joins, especially FULL JOIN, can be resource-intensive on large datasets. Use them judiciously and consider indexing join columns to improve performance.

Section 6.5: Summary and What's Next

In this chapter, you learned about joining tables using INNER JOIN, LEFT JOIN, RIGHT JOIN, and FULL JOIN. You also saw practical applications for each join type in generating comprehensive sales reports and worked through exercises to practice these concepts.

In the next chapter, we'll explore data aggregation functions, such as COUNT, SUM, AVG, MIN, and MAX, which are often used with joins to generate summaries and insights. With these tools, you'll gain even greater control over your data analysis in SQL.

Let's move forward and continue building your SQL skills!

Chapter 7: Aggregating Data with COUNT, SUM, AVG, MIN, MAX

Welcome to Chapter 7! In this chapter, we'll dive into SQL's aggregation functions—COUNT, SUM, AVG, MIN, and MAX. These functions allow you to summarize data and gain insights that go beyond individual rows, helping you answer questions such as "How many orders were placed?" or "What is the average transaction size?" By the end of this chapter, you'll know how to use these functions effectively and apply them to real-world scenarios.

Section 7.1: Understanding Aggregate Functions in SQL

Aggregate functions perform calculations across a set of values, often returning a single summarized result. Here's a quick overview of the most commonly used aggregate functions:

1. **COUNT**: Counts the number of rows or non-NULL values in a column.

2. **SUM**: Adds up the values in a column (used with numeric data).

3. **AVG**: Calculates the average value of a column (used with numeric data).

4. **MIN**: Finds the smallest value in a column.

5. **MAX**: Finds the largest value in a column.

Aggregate functions are typically used with the GROUP BY clause, which we covered in the previous chapter, to organize results by category.

Section 7.2: Using COUNT to Count Rows or Values

The COUNT function is used to count the number of rows that meet a certain condition or count non-NULL values in a column. Here are two common ways to use COUNT:

- **COUNT(*)**: Counts all rows, including those with NULL values.
- **COUNT(column_name)**: Counts only non-NULL values in a specific column.

Example: Counting the number of orders in the Orders table.

sql

Copy code

```
SELECT COUNT(*) AS TotalOrders
FROM Orders;
```

This query returns the total number of rows in the Orders table. If you wanted to count only rows where the Amount column is not NULL, you would use COUNT(Amount) instead.

Section 7.3: Using SUM to Calculate Total Sales

The SUM function calculates the total of all values in a specified column, making it especially useful for financial data.

Example: Calculating total sales in the Orders table.

sql

Copy code

SELECT SUM(Amount) AS TotalSales

FROM Orders;

This query adds up all the values in the Amount column to give the total sales figure. It's a valuable metric for understanding overall business performance.

Section 7.4: Using AVG to Find the Average Transaction Size

The AVG function calculates the average of all values in a numeric column, giving you insights like average order amount or average customer age.

Example: Calculating the average transaction size.

sql

Copy code

SELECT AVG(Amount) AS AverageTransaction

FROM Orders;

This query calculates the average value of the Amount column, providing the average transaction size. This metric can be useful for setting sales targets or understanding customer spending habits.

Section 7.5: Using MIN and MAX to Find Minimum and Maximum Values

The MIN and MAX functions help you find the smallest and largest values in a column. They're useful for identifying things like the lowest and highest transaction amounts.

Example: Finding the smallest and largest transaction amounts.

sql

Copy code

```sql
SELECT MIN(Amount) AS SmallestTransaction, MAX(Amount) AS LargestTransaction
FROM Orders;
```

This query returns the smallest and largest values in the Amount column, which can help you understand the range of transaction sizes.

Section 7.6: Real-World Example – Calculating Total Sales and Average Transaction Size

Let's apply these aggregate functions to a real-world scenario. Imagine a retail business that wants to review sales performance by calculating total sales and the average transaction size. The Orders table contains the following columns: OrderID, CustomerID, OrderDate, and Amount.

Step 1: Calculating Total Sales

To calculate total sales, use the SUM function:

sql

```
SELECT SUM(Amount) AS TotalSales
FROM Orders;
```

This query adds up all values in the Amount column, providing the total sales figure. If you wanted to calculate total sales within a specific time frame, you could add a WHERE clause to filter by date.

Step 2: Calculating Average Transaction Size

To find the average transaction size, use the AVG function:

sql

```
SELECT AVG(Amount) AS AverageTransaction
FROM Orders;
```

This query returns the average amount spent per transaction, which helps the business understand customer spending patterns.

Step 3: Calculating Monthly Sales Using GROUP BY

If the business wants to see total sales for each month, use GROUP BY in combination with SUM to aggregate data by month.

sql

```
SELECT DATE_FORMAT(OrderDate, '%Y-%m') AS Month,
SUM(Amount) AS TotalMonthlySales
FROM Orders
GROUP BY Month
ORDER BY Month ASC;
```

This query uses GROUP BY to summarize sales by month, providing a monthly breakdown of total sales.

Section 7.7: Sample Queries with Aggregation Functions

Let's try some sample queries to reinforce your understanding of aggregation functions.

Exercise 1: Count the Number of Customers

1. **Goal**: Retrieve the total number of customers in the Customers table.
2. **Expected Output**: A single number representing the total count of customers.
3. **Solution**:

sql
```
SELECT COUNT(*) AS TotalCustomers
FROM Customers;
```

Exercise 2: Calculate Total Sales Above a Specific Amount

1. **Goal**: Calculate the total sales for orders where the amount is above $100.
2. **Expected Output**: The total sales amount for high-value transactions.
3. **Solution**:

sql

```sql
SELECT SUM(Amount) AS TotalHighValueSales
FROM Orders
WHERE Amount > 100;
```

Exercise 3: Find the Average Order Amount per Customer

1. **Goal**: Calculate the average order amount for each customer in the Orders table.
2. **Expected Output**: A list of customers and their average order amounts.
3. **Solution**:

```sql
sql
SELECT        CustomerID,        AVG(Amount)        AS
AverageOrderAmount
FROM Orders
GROUP BY CustomerID;
```

Exercise 4: Identify Highest and Lowest Transactions

1. **Goal**: Retrieve the highest and lowest transaction amounts from the Orders table.
2. **Expected Output**: Two numbers representing the smallest and largest order amounts.
3. **Solution**:

```sql
sql
```

SELECT   MIN(Amount)   AS   SmallestTransaction,
MAX(Amount) AS LargestTransaction
FROM Orders;

Section 7.8: Common Mistakes and Best Practices with Aggregate Functions

Here are some common mistakes to avoid when using aggregate functions, along with best practices:

1. **Avoid Using Aggregate Functions Without GROUP BY (If Needed)**: When using aggregate functions with GROUP BY, ensure each column not in an aggregate function is included in the GROUP BY clause. Failure to do so will cause SQL errors or unexpected results.

2. **Check for NULL Values**: Aggregate functions like SUM, AVG, MIN, and MAX ignore NULL values, but COUNT can include them if you use COUNT(*). Be mindful of how NULL values might affect your results.

3. **Alias Columns for Readability**: Use aliases (e.g., AS TotalSales) to make your query results easier to understand, especially in reports or complex queries.

4. **Filter Data Before Aggregating (If Necessary)**: Use WHERE before GROUP BY to filter data before aggregating it. Filtering afterward may not be possible with aggregate functions.

    ○ **Example**: To calculate total sales above $100 per month, first filter with WHERE Amount > 100, then group by month.

5. **Using HAVING for Post-Aggregation Filtering**: To filter results based on aggregated values, use HAVING after GROUP BY.

    ○ **Example**:

sql

SELECT   CustomerID,   SUM(Amount)   AS TotalSpent

FROM Orders

GROUP BY CustomerID

HAVING TotalSpent > 500;

This query returns only customers with total spending over $500.

Section 7.9: Summary and What's Next

In this chapter, you learned how to use SQL's aggregation functions—COUNT, SUM, AVG, MIN, and MAX—to summarize and gain insights from data. You practiced calculating metrics like total sales and average transaction size and completed exercises to reinforce your understanding of these functions.

Next, in Chapter 8, we'll explore how to manipulate data with SQL commands like INSERT, UPDATE, and DELETE. These commands allow you to add, modify, and remove data in tables, essential skills for managing data dynamically in any database.

Let's keep building on your SQL knowledge and skills!

CHAPTER 8: INSERTING, UPDATING, AND DELETING DATA

In this chapter, we'll cover three core SQL commands for managing data: INSERT, UPDATE, and DELETE. These commands allow you to add new records, modify existing data, and remove unwanted records from tables. Each command is essential for maintaining a dynamic database where data can be managed, updated, and removed as needed. We'll explore real-world examples like updating inventory levels and deleting outdated records, and discuss techniques to ensure data integrity.

Section 8.1: Using the INSERT Command

The INSERT command is used to add new records (rows) to a table. When inserting data, it's important to know which columns you need to populate and ensure that the values align with the table's structure and data types.

The basic syntax for INSERT is:

```sql
Copy code
INSERT INTO table_name (column1, column2, ...)
VALUES (value1, value2, ...);
```

- **table_name**: The name of the table where you're adding data.

- **column1, column2, ...**: Specifies the columns you're adding data to.

- **VALUES**: Introduces the values to be inserted in the specified columns.

Example: Adding a new product to an inventory.

Assume we have an `Inventory` table with columns `ProductID`, `ProductName`, `Quantity`, and `Price`. Here's how to add a new product:

```sql
Copy code
INSERT INTO Inventory (ProductID, ProductName,
Quantity, Price)
VALUES (101, 'Coffee Beans', 50, 9.99);
```

This command adds a new row to the `Inventory` table, creating an entry for "Coffee Beans" with an initial stock of 50 units at a price of $9.99.

Section 8.2: Using the UPDATE Command

The `UPDATE` command is used to modify existing records in a table. It allows you to change specific values based on certain conditions, making it essential for maintaining accurate data as information changes over time.

The basic syntax for `UPDATE` is:

```sql
Copy code
```

```
UPDATE table_name
SET column1 = value1, column2 = value2, ...
WHERE condition;
```

- **SET**: Specifies the columns to update and the new values to assign.

- **WHERE**: Specifies a condition to ensure that only the desired rows are updated. Without WHERE, all rows in the table would be updated.

Example: Updating inventory levels for a product.

Suppose the stock for "Coffee Beans" (ProductID = 101) has decreased after a few sales. Here's how to update the quantity:

```
sql
Copy code
UPDATE Inventory
SET Quantity = Quantity - 5
WHERE ProductID = 101;
```

This command reduces the Quantity of "Coffee Beans" by 5, adjusting the stock to reflect recent sales. The WHERE clause ensures that only the row with ProductID = 101 is updated.

Section 8.3: Using the DELETE Command

The DELETE command removes records from a table based on a specified condition. Be careful when using DELETE, as it permanently removes data. Always use the WHERE clause to limit deletion to specific rows; without WHERE, all rows in the table will be deleted.

The basic syntax for DELETE is:

```sql
Copy code
DELETE FROM table_name
WHERE condition;
```

- **DELETE FROM**: Identifies the table from which you want to delete rows.
- **WHERE**: Limits deletion to rows meeting a specific condition.

Example: Deleting outdated records from inventory.

Suppose a product has been discontinued and needs to be removed from the Inventory table. Here's how to delete it:

```sql
DELETE FROM Inventory
WHERE ProductID = 101;
```

This command removes the row with ProductID = 101 from the Inventory table. Without the WHERE clause, all records in the Inventory table would be deleted.

Section 8.4: Real-World Example – Updating Inventory Levels and Deleting Outdated Records

Let's apply INSERT, UPDATE, and DELETE commands in a real-world inventory management scenario for a retail business.

Step 1: Adding New Products to Inventory

When the business receives new stock, they can add each product to the Inventory table. Suppose the business adds a new product, "Tea Bags," with 100 units in stock at $5.99 each.

```sql
Copy code
INSERT INTO Inventory (ProductID, ProductName,
Quantity, Price)
VALUES (102, 'Tea Bags', 100, 5.99);
```

This command creates a new entry in the Inventory table, adding "Tea Bags" with the specified quantity and price.

Step 2: Updating Inventory Levels After Sales

As products are sold, the inventory levels need to be updated to reflect the remaining stock. Let's assume that 10 units of "Tea Bags" were sold.

```sql
UPDATE Inventory
SET Quantity = Quantity - 10
WHERE ProductID = 102;
```

This query reduces the Quantity of "Tea Bags" by 10, ensuring that the database accurately reflects current stock levels.

Step 3: Removing Discontinued Products

If the business decides to stop selling a product, they may want to remove it from the inventory to keep the database organized and up-to-date. Suppose "Tea Bags" is discontinued:

```sql
DELETE FROM Inventory
WHERE ProductID = 102;
```

This command removes the "Tea Bags" entry from the `Inventory` table. It's important to use WHERE to prevent accidentally deleting all rows.

Section 8.5: Ensuring Data Integrity with Practical Examples

When inserting, updating, or deleting data, maintaining data integrity is critical to avoid errors and inconsistencies. Here are some practical techniques to ensure data integrity when using INSERT, UPDATE, and DELETE.

1. Using Primary Keys and Unique Constraints

To prevent duplicate records, use primary keys and unique constraints. For example, if `ProductID` is a primary key in the `Inventory` table, SQL will prevent duplicate entries with the same `ProductID`.

```sql
CREATE TABLE Inventory (
    ProductID INT PRIMARY KEY,
    ProductName VARCHAR(50),
    Quantity INT,
    Price DECIMAL(10, 2)
);
```

2. Setting Default Values

Define default values for certain columns so that missing information doesn't disrupt data entry. For example, you could set a default `Quantity` of 0 for products that are initially out of stock.

```sql
ALTER TABLE Inventory
MODIFY Quantity INT DEFAULT 0;
```

3. Using Transactions for Safe Updates

Transactions allow you to group multiple SQL commands into a single unit of work, ensuring that all commands succeed or none at all. This is especially useful if your updates involve multiple tables or rows. Use BEGIN, COMMIT, and ROLLBACK for transaction control.

Example: Ensuring a safe update of inventory levels.

```sql
BEGIN;

UPDATE Inventory
SET Quantity = Quantity - 10
WHERE ProductID = 101;

IF Quantity < 0 THEN
    ROLLBACK;   -- Cancel if inventory falls below 0
ELSE
    COMMIT;
END IF;
```

If any part of this transaction fails (e.g., trying to set Quantity below 0), the ROLLBACK command cancels the transaction, keeping your data consistent.

4. Using WHERE Clauses to Target Specific Rows

Always use WHERE clauses with UPDATE and DELETE commands to prevent accidental modifications or deletions of all rows.

- **Correct**:

  ```sql
  DELETE FROM Inventory WHERE ProductID = 101;
  ```

- **Incorrect**:

```sql
DELETE FROM Inventory;
```

Without WHERE, the DELETE command removes all rows, which can be a costly mistake in production.

Section 8.6: Practice Exercises with INSERT, UPDATE, and DELETE

Try these exercises to practice using INSERT, UPDATE, and DELETE commands effectively.

Exercise 1: Adding New Customer Data

1. **Goal**: Add a new customer to the Customers table.
2. **Expected Output**: A new row with customer information.
3. **Solution**:

```sql
Copy code
INSERT INTO Customers (CustomerID, Name, Email,
Phone)
VALUES (201, 'Alice Johnson',
'alice@example.com', '555-6789');
```

Exercise 2: Updating Product Prices

1. **Goal**: Increase the price of all products in the Inventory table by 5%.
2. **Expected Output**: Each product's Price increased by 5%.
3. **Solution**:

```sql
UPDATE Inventory
SET Price = Price * 1.05;
```

Exercise 3: Removing Records for Expired Products

1. **Goal**: Delete all products from the `Inventory` table where `Quantity` is 0.
2. **Expected Output**: All out-of-stock products removed from the inventory.
3. **Solution**:

```sql
DELETE FROM Inventory
WHERE Quantity = 0;
```

Exercise 4: Safe Inventory Update with Transaction

1. **Goal**: Reduce inventory for a specific product only if enough stock is available.
2. **Solution**:

```sql
BEGIN;

UPDATE Inventory
SET Quantity = Quantity - 20
WHERE ProductID = 101;

IF Quantity >= 0 THEN
    COMMIT;
ELSE
    ROLLBACK;
END IF;
```

This transaction ensures that inventory isn't reduced if it would result in negative stock.

Section 8.7: Summary and What's Next

In this chapter, you learned how to use the INSERT, UPDATE, and DELETE commands to manage data dynamically in SQL. We covered practical applications, such as updating inventory and deleting outdated records, and discussed methods to ensure data integrity.

In the next chapter, we'll explore subqueries and nested queries, which will allow you to write more flexible and powerful SQL queries by embedding one query within another.

Great work so far! Let's keep moving forward on your path to SQL mastery.

CHAPTER 9: SUB QUERIES AND NESTED QUERIES

Welcome to Chapter 9! In this chapter, we'll explore subqueries, or nested queries, which allow you to embed one query within another. Subqueries enable you to break down complex queries into smaller, manageable parts, making it easier to extract specific data from multiple tables. By the end of this chapter, you'll know how to use subqueries effectively and apply them in real-world scenarios, such as finding top customers based on purchase amounts.

Section 9.1: Introduction to Subqueries

A **subquery** is a query embedded within another query. Subqueries are enclosed in parentheses and typically provide results to the main, or "outer," query. Subqueries can be used in various places within a SQL statement, including in the SELECT, FROM, and WHERE clauses. By simplifying the structure of a complex query, subqueries make data retrieval more flexible and adaptable.

There are two main types of subqueries:

1. **Single-row subqueries**: Return one row, often used with operators like =, <, >, etc.
2. **Multi-row subqueries**: Return multiple rows, commonly used with operators like IN, ANY, or ALL.

Example: Suppose you want to find the highest order amount in the Orders table. A basic subquery could look like this:

```sql
Copy code
SELECT MAX(Amount)
FROM Orders;
```

Now imagine that we want to find the customer(s) who placed the highest order. This task would involve a subquery to first find the highest order amount and then return the details of customers with that order.

```sql
Copy code
SELECT CustomerID, OrderID, Amount
FROM Orders
WHERE Amount = (SELECT MAX(Amount) FROM Orders);
```

Here, the subquery (SELECT MAX(Amount) FROM Orders) finds the highest order amount, and the outer query retrieves the CustomerID and OrderID for that amount.

Section 9.2: Types of Subqueries and Their Uses

Subqueries can be used in various parts of a SQL statement. Here's a breakdown of some of the most common uses.

1. Subqueries in the WHERE Clause

Using a subquery in the WHERE clause is one of the most common approaches. It allows you to filter data based on the result of another query.

Example: Finding orders with amounts above the average.

```sql
Copy code
SELECT OrderID, CustomerID, Amount
```

```
FROM Orders
WHERE Amount > (SELECT AVG(Amount) FROM Orders);
```

This query finds orders where the `Amount` is greater than the average order amount, determined by the subquery `(SELECT AVG(Amount)` `FROM Orders)`.

2. Subqueries in the FROM Clause

Subqueries in the `FROM` clause are often called "inline views." This type of subquery can act as a temporary table that you can join with other tables or use to further filter data.

Example: Calculating the total sales for each customer and then filtering for high-spending customers.

```sql
Copy code
SELECT CustomerID, TotalSpent
FROM (SELECT CustomerID, SUM(Amount) AS TotalSpent
      FROM Orders
      GROUP BY CustomerID) AS CustomerSales
WHERE TotalSpent > 500;
```

In this query, the subquery in the `FROM` clause calculates the total amount each customer has spent. The outer query then filters these results to only show customers who spent more than $500.

3. Subqueries in the SELECT Clause

Subqueries in the `SELECT` clause allow you to compute additional values for each row in the result.

Example: Finding each order's total amount and comparing it to the overall average.

```sql
```

```
Copy code
SELECT OrderID, Amount,
       (SELECT AVG(Amount) FROM Orders) AS
AverageOrder
FROM Orders;
```

In this query, the subquery (SELECT AVG(Amount) FROM Orders) calculates the overall average order amount, and the outer query includes this average in each row.

Section 9.3: Real-World Application – Finding Top Customers Based on Purchase Amounts

To see subqueries in action, let's consider a scenario where a business wants to find its top customers based on the total amount spent. The Orders table includes columns for OrderID, CustomerID, and Amount, while the Customers table has columns for CustomerID, Name, and Email.

Step 1: Calculating Total Amount Spent by Each Customer

First, we'll use a subquery to calculate the total spending per customer.

```sql
Copy code
SELECT CustomerID, SUM(Amount) AS TotalSpent
FROM Orders
GROUP BY CustomerID;
```

This query provides a list of each customer's total spending. To find only the top customers, we need to filter this list based on a certain threshold, like the average total spending.

Step 2: Filtering for Top-Spending Customers

We can create a final query that retrieves only those customers who have spent above the average amount. The average can be calculated using a subquery.

```sql
Copy code
SELECT CustomerID, TotalSpent
FROM (SELECT CustomerID, SUM(Amount) AS TotalSpent
        FROM Orders
        GROUP BY CustomerID) AS CustomerTotals
WHERE TotalSpent > (SELECT AVG(TotalSpent)
                        FROM (SELECT SUM(Amount) AS
TotalSpent
                            FROM Orders
                            GROUP BY CustomerID) AS
AvgTotal);
```

In this example:

1. **The inner subquery** (SELECT SUM(Amount) AS TotalSpent FROM Orders GROUP BY CustomerID) **calculates total spending per customer.**
2. **The outer query** (SELECT AVG(TotalSpent) FROM ...) **calculates the average spending.**
3. **The main query filters customers who spent above this average.**

Section 9.4: Writing Queries Within Queries for Flexible Data Extraction

Subqueries allow for powerful and flexible data extraction. Here are some common scenarios where subqueries can simplify your work.

1. Identifying Customers with No Orders

A subquery can help identify customers who have never placed an order. In this case, we would look for customers whose `CustomerID` does not appear in the `Orders` table.

```sql
Copy code
SELECT Name
FROM Customers
WHERE CustomerID NOT IN (SELECT CustomerID FROM
Orders);
```

This query uses a subquery to find `CustomerID`s in the `Orders` table and then returns only those `CustomerID`s from the `Customers` table that don't have a match.

2. Finding the Most Recent Orders for Each Customer

If you want to find the most recent order for each customer, a subquery can identify the latest order date.

```sql
Copy code
SELECT CustomerID, OrderID, OrderDate, Amount
FROM Orders
WHERE OrderDate = (SELECT MAX(OrderDate)
                   FROM Orders AS SubOrders
                   WHERE SubOrders.CustomerID =
Orders.CustomerID);
```

In this query, the subquery (`SELECT MAX(OrderDate) FROM Orders WHERE` ...) finds the most recent order date for each `CustomerID`, allowing you to retrieve each customer's latest order.

3. Comparing Each Row to an Aggregate Result

Subqueries can also be useful for comparing each row in a table to an aggregate result. For example, you can identify orders that are above the overall average.

```sql
Copy code
SELECT OrderID, Amount
FROM Orders
WHERE Amount > (SELECT AVG(Amount) FROM Orders);
```

This query uses a subquery to calculate the average amount, filtering the results to show only those orders where Amount is above average.

Section 9.5: Practice Exercises with Subqueries

Let's practice subqueries with some real-world scenarios.

Exercise 1: Identify Low-Spending Customers

1. **Goal**: Find customers whose total spending is below the average.
2. **Expected Output**: A list of CustomerIDs and total amounts for low-spending customers.
3. **Solution**:

```sql
Copy code
SELECT CustomerID, TotalSpent
FROM (SELECT CustomerID, SUM(Amount) AS
TotalSpent
      FROM Orders
      GROUP BY CustomerID) AS CustomerTotals
WHERE TotalSpent < (SELECT AVG(TotalSpent)
                    FROM (SELECT SUM(Amount) AS
TotalSpent
                          FROM Orders
                          GROUP BY CustomerID)
AS AvgTotal);
```

Exercise 2: Retrieve Products Not Ordered in the Last 30 Days

1. **Goal**: Find products from the Products table that have not been ordered in the last 30 days.
2. **Expected Output**: A list of ProductIDs that haven't been ordered recently.

3. **Solution**:

```sql
Copy code
SELECT ProductID, ProductName
FROM Products
WHERE ProductID NOT IN (SELECT ProductID
                        FROM Orders
                        WHERE OrderDate >=
DATE_SUB(CURDATE(), INTERVAL 30 DAY));
```

Exercise 3: Find Orders with Above-Average Quantity

1. **Goal**: Retrieve all orders with quantities above the average.
2. **Expected Output**: A list of OrderIDs and quantities that are above average.
3. **Solution**:

```sql
Copy code
SELECT OrderID, Quantity
FROM OrderItems
WHERE Quantity > (SELECT AVG(Quantity) FROM
OrderItems);
```

Section 9.6: Common Mistakes and Best Practices with Subqueries

Here are some best practices for using subqueries effectively:

1. **Use Aliases for Clarity**: Assign aliases to subqueries to make complex queries easier to read, especially when joining subqueries with other tables.
2. **Optimize with EXISTS and IN**: When filtering based on the existence of a condition, use EXISTS or IN instead of joining subqueries. EXISTS can be more efficient in certain cases.
   o **Example**:

```sql
Copy code
SELECT Name
FROM Customers
WHERE EXISTS (SELECT 1 FROM Orders WHERE
Orders.CustomerID =
Customers.CustomerID);
```

3. **Check for NULL Values**: Ensure that your subqueries account for potential NULL values, especially when using IN or NOT IN operators.
4. **Test Subqueries Separately**: Run subqueries independently first to verify their output before combining them into the main query.

Section 9.7: Summary and What's Next

In this chapter, you learned how to use subqueries to simplify complex queries and gain more flexibility in data extraction. We covered different types of subqueries, such as those in the WHERE, FROM, and SELECT clauses, and saw practical applications like finding top customers based on spending.

In the next chapter, we'll explore advanced filtering techniques with SQL commands like LIKE, IN, BETWEEN, and handling NULL values to refine your queries further.

Great job on learning subqueries—this skill will be valuable as you tackle more complex SQL tasks!

CHAPTER 10: ADVANCED FILTERING WITH LIKE, IN, BETWEEN, AND NULL HANDLING

Welcome to Chapter 10! In this chapter, we'll cover advanced filtering techniques in SQL using commands like LIKE, IN, BETWEEN, and methods for handling NULL values. These tools help you refine your queries by allowing pattern matching, range-based filtering, and list-based filtering. By the end of this chapter, you'll be able to build highly specific queries and handle common data challenges such as filtering incomplete data or working with different data formats.

Section 10.1: Pattern Matching with LIKE

The LIKE operator is used to search for a specified pattern in a column. It's especially useful for filtering text data when you need to find partial matches rather than exact values. LIKE works with two wildcard characters:

1. %: Represents zero, one, or multiple characters.
2. _: Represents a single character.

The basic syntax for LIKE is:

```sql
Copy code
SELECT column1, column2, ...
FROM table_name
WHERE column_name LIKE pattern;
```

Example: Finding customers whose names start with "A."

```sql
Copy code
SELECT Name, Email
FROM Customers
WHERE Name LIKE 'A%';
```

This query returns all customers whose names begin with the letter

"A." The % wildcard matches any number of characters after "A."

Additional Examples with LIKE

1. **Finding email addresses from a specific domain**:

    ```sql
    Copy code
    SELECT Name, Email
    FROM Customers
    WHERE Email LIKE '%@gmail.com';
    ```

    This query retrieves all customers with email addresses

    ending in @gmail.com.

2. **Searching for names with exactly five characters**:

    ```sql
    Copy code
    SELECT Name
    FROM Customers
    WHERE Name LIKE '_____';
    ```

    Here, _____ (five underscores) specifies names with exactly

    five characters.

Section 10.2: List-Based Filtering with IN

The IN operator allows you to filter data based on a list of possible

values. This is helpful when you want to match multiple values in a

single column without writing multiple OR conditions.

The basic syntax for IN is:

```sql
Copy code
SELECT column1, column2, ...
FROM table_name
WHERE column_name IN (value1, value2, ...);
```

Example: Retrieving customers from specific states.

```sql
Copy code
SELECT Name, State
FROM Customers
WHERE State IN ('California', 'New York', 'Texas');
```

This query retrieves only the customers from California, New York,

or Texas.

Additional Examples with IN

1. **Finding orders with specific statuses**:

   ```sql
   Copy code
   SELECT OrderID, Status
   FROM Orders
   WHERE Status IN ('Pending', 'Shipped',
   'Completed');
   ```

   This query retrieves orders that are currently pending,

   shipped, or completed.

2. **Combining IN with a Subquery**:

   ```sql
   Copy code
   SELECT Name
   FROM Customers
   WHERE CustomerID IN (SELECT CustomerID FROM
   Orders WHERE Amount > 100);
   ```

Here, IN is used with a subquery to retrieve customers who have placed orders over $100.

Section 10.3: Range-Based Filtering with BETWEEN

The BETWEEN operator allows you to filter data within a specified range. It's commonly used for date or numeric data but can also work with text (for alphabetical ranges).

The basic syntax for BETWEEN is:

```sql
Copy code
SELECT column1, column2, ...
FROM table_name
WHERE column_name BETWEEN value1 AND value2;
```

Example: Retrieving orders within a specific date range.

```sql
Copy code
SELECT OrderID, OrderDate, Amount
FROM Orders
WHERE OrderDate BETWEEN '2023-01-01' AND '2023-12-31';
```

This query retrieves all orders placed in 2023.

Additional Examples with BETWEEN

1. **Filtering by numerical ranges**:

   ```sql
   Copy code
   SELECT ProductName, Price
   FROM Products
   WHERE Price BETWEEN 10 AND 50;
   ```

   This query finds products with prices between $10 and $50.

2. **Finding customers based on age range**:

```sql
Copy code
SELECT Name, Age
FROM Customers
WHERE Age BETWEEN 20 AND 30;
```

Here, BETWEEN is used to retrieve customers aged between 20 and 30, inclusive.

Section 10.4: Handling NULL Values

NULL represents missing or undefined data in SQL. Since NULL isn't a value but rather an absence of value, you must use specific functions to handle NULL in queries. Common operations for handling NULL include:

1. **IS NULL**: Checks if a column has NULL values.
2. **IS NOT NULL**: Checks if a column has non-NULL values.

The basic syntax for IS NULL and IS NOT NULL is:

```sql
Copy code
SELECT column1, column2, ...
FROM table_name
WHERE column_name IS NULL;
```

Example: Finding customers without email addresses.

```sql
Copy code
SELECT Name
FROM Customers
WHERE Email IS NULL;
```

This query retrieves customers whose Email field is NULL, indicating they haven't provided an email address.

Using COALESCE to Handle NULL Values

The COALESCE function returns the first non-NULL value in a list of expressions. It's useful for providing default values in place of NULL.

Example: Displaying "Not Available" for customers with missing phone numbers.

```sql
Copy code
SELECT Name, COALESCE(Phone, 'Not Available') AS
ContactNumber
FROM Customers;
```

This query replaces any NULL values in the Phone column with the text "Not Available."

Section 10.5: Real-World Examples with Customer Demographics and Order Status Queries

To see how these filtering techniques work together, let's look at practical examples based on customer demographics and order statuses.

Example 1: Finding Customers in a Specific Age Range with Partial Name Match

Suppose a business wants to target customers aged between 25 and 40 whose names begin with "J."

```sql
Copy code
SELECT Name, Age, Email
FROM Customers
WHERE Age BETWEEN 25 AND 40
  AND Name LIKE 'J%';
```

This query combines BETWEEN and LIKE to retrieve only customers aged 25 to 40 with names starting with "J."

Example 2: Retrieving Orders by Status and Date Range

Imagine the company wants a list of completed or shipped orders placed in the last 6 months.

```sql
Copy code
SELECT OrderID, OrderDate, Status
FROM Orders
WHERE Status IN ('Completed', 'Shipped')
  AND OrderDate BETWEEN DATE_SUB(CURDATE(), INTERVAL
6 MONTH) AND CURDATE();
```

This query combines IN and BETWEEN to retrieve orders that have a status of "Completed" or "Shipped" and were placed within the last six months.

Example 3: Identifying Incomplete Customer Data

To identify customers with missing email or phone information, you can use IS NULL.

```sql
Copy code
SELECT Name, Email, Phone
FROM Customers
WHERE Email IS NULL OR Phone IS NULL;
```

This query returns customers who haven't provided either an email or a phone number, useful for data completeness checks.

Section 10.6: Practice Exercises with Advanced Filtering

Let's practice these filtering techniques with some sample exercises.

Exercise 1: Retrieve Customers with Specific Name Patterns

1. **Goal**: Find customers whose names contain "son."
2. **Expected Output**: A list of customer names with "son" anywhere in the name.

3. **Solution**:

```sql
Copy code
SELECT Name
FROM Customers
WHERE Name LIKE '%son%';
```

Exercise 2: List Orders for a Set of Specific Customers

1. **Goal**: Retrieve orders placed by customers with
   CustomerID values of 1, 3, and 5.
2. **Expected Output**: A list of orders for those specific
   customers.
3. **Solution**:

```sql
Copy code
SELECT OrderID, CustomerID, Amount
FROM Orders
WHERE CustomerID IN (1, 3, 5);
```

Exercise 3: Find High-Value Orders Placed in a Specific Range

1. **Goal**: Find orders with amounts between $100 and $500.
2. **Expected Output**: A list of orders with Amount values in
   the specified range.
3. **Solution**:

```sql
Copy code
SELECT OrderID, Amount
FROM Orders
WHERE Amount BETWEEN 100 AND 500;
```

Exercise 4: Identify Customers with Missing Data

1. **Goal**: Retrieve a list of customers with missing phone
   numbers.

2. **Expected Output**: A list of customer names with NULL phone numbers.
3. **Solution**:

```sql
Copy code
SELECT Name
FROM Customers
WHERE Phone IS NULL;
```

Section 10.7: Common Mistakes and Best Practices with Advanced Filtering

1. **Be Cautious with LIKE Patterns**: Be careful when using % in LIKE queries, as it can return large result sets. Use specific patterns when possible.
2. **Use IN for Multiple Values**: Instead of multiple OR statements, use IN for simpler syntax and improved readability.
3. **Remember to Handle NULL Explicitly**: Using = with NULL doesn't work; use IS NULL or IS NOT NULL instead to correctly filter NULL values.
4. **Combine Multiple Filters Thoughtfully**: When combining LIKE, IN, BETWEEN, and NULL handling, use parentheses and check for logical consistency to ensure the query returns accurate results.

Section 10.8: Summary and What's Next

In this chapter, you learned how to use advanced filtering techniques in SQL with LIKE, IN, BETWEEN, and NULL handling. These techniques allow you to create more specific queries, enabling you to extract precisely the data you need for real-world scenarios.

In the next chapter, we'll explore working with dates and times, focusing on SQL functions to manipulate, calculate, and format date and time data. This skill will be valuable for queries involving time-sensitive information, like order dates or customer anniversaries.

CHAPTER 11: WORKING WITH DATES AND TIMES

Welcome to Chapter 11! In this chapter, we'll cover how to work with dates and times in SQL, a valuable skill for handling data related to order dates, delivery timelines, and retention periods. SQL provides several functions to extract, manipulate, and calculate date and time values. By the end of this chapter, you'll be comfortable using SQL's date and time functions, and you'll practice applying them in real-world scenarios.

Section 11.1: SQL Functions for Managing Dates and Times

SQL offers several functions to help you work with date and time data effectively. Here are some of the most commonly used date and time functions:

1. **CURRENT_DATE**: Returns the current date (without the time).
2. **CURRENT_TIMESTAMP**: Returns the current date and time.
3. **DATE()**: Extracts the date portion from a date-time value.
4. **YEAR(), MONTH(), DAY()**: Extracts the year, month, or day from a date.
5. **DATEDIFF()**: Calculates the difference in days between two dates.

6. **DATE_ADD()** / **DATE_SUB()**: Adds or subtracts a specified time interval to/from a date.

7. **DATE_FORMAT()**: Formats a date based on a specified pattern.

These functions allow you to retrieve current date information, manipulate dates by adding or subtracting days, and format date values to display them as needed.

Section 11.2: Extracting Specific Date Parts

SQL's date functions allow you to extract parts of a date (like the year, month, or day) to make it easier to group, filter, or analyze date-based data.

Extracting the Year, Month, and Day

To extract the year, month, or day from a date, you can use the `YEAR()`, `MONTH()`, and `DAY()` functions.

Example: Extracting the year, month, and day from an order date.

```sql
Copy code
SELECT OrderID, OrderDate, YEAR(OrderDate) AS
OrderYear, MONTH(OrderDate) AS OrderMonth,
DAY(OrderDate) AS OrderDay
FROM Orders;
```

This query retrieves the year, month, and day of each `OrderDate`, making it easier to group or filter orders by specific periods.

Calculating Date Differences with DATEDIFF()

The DATEDIFF() function calculates the number of days between two dates. This is useful for tracking timelines, such as calculating the number of days between an order and its delivery.

Example: Finding the number of days since each order was placed.

```sql
Copy code
SELECT OrderID, OrderDate, DATEDIFF(CURRENT_DATE,
OrderDate) AS DaysSinceOrder
FROM Orders;
```

This query calculates the days elapsed since each order date, allowing you to identify older orders that may need follow-up.

Section 11.3: Manipulating Dates with DATE_ADD and DATE_SUB

DATE_ADD and DATE_SUB allow you to add or subtract intervals from a date. You can use these functions to calculate future or past dates, such as estimated delivery dates or expiration dates.

Adding Days, Months, or Years to a Date

The DATE_ADD() function allows you to add a specified interval to a date.

Example: Calculating estimated delivery dates 7 days after the order date.

```sql
SELECT OrderID, OrderDate, DATE_ADD(OrderDate,
INTERVAL 7 DAY) AS EstimatedDeliveryDate
FROM Orders;
```

This query calculates a delivery date 7 days after each order date, providing a timeline for delivery expectations.

Subtracting Days, Months, or Years from a Date

The DATE_SUB() function allows you to subtract a specified interval from a date.

Example: Finding customers who have been inactive for over a year.

```sql
Copy code
SELECT CustomerID, LastOrderDate
FROM Customers
WHERE LastOrderDate < DATE_SUB(CURRENT_DATE, INTERVAL
1 YEAR);
```

This query identifies customers who haven't placed an order in over a year, which is useful for targeted marketing efforts to re-engage inactive customers.

Section 11.4: Formatting Dates with DATE_FORMAT

DATE_FORMAT() allows you to display date values in specific formats, making it easier to prepare data for reports or to match particular date formats.

The basic syntax for DATE_FORMAT() is:

```sql
DATE_FORMAT(date_column, 'format')
```

Example: Formatting order dates as MM-DD-YYYY.

```sql
Copy code
SELECT OrderID, DATE_FORMAT(OrderDate, '%m-%d-%Y') AS
FormattedOrderDate
FROM Orders;
```

This query reformats OrderDate to display in MM-DD-YYYY format, making it more readable for certain audiences.

Common date format specifiers:

- `%Y`: Year (4 digits)
- `%y`: Year (2 digits)
- `%m`: Month (2 digits)
- `%d`: Day (2 digits)
- `%H`: Hour (24-hour format)
- `%i`: Minutes
- `%s`: Seconds

Section 11.5: Real-World Example – Tracking Order Dates, Delivery Timelines, and Retention Periods

To see these date functions in action, let's consider a scenario where a business wants to track order timelines, estimate delivery dates, and identify retention periods.

Step 1: Calculating Days Since Each Order

The business wants to monitor how many days have passed since each order was placed to prioritize follow-ups for older orders.

```sql
Copy code
SELECT OrderID, OrderDate, DATEDIFF(CURRENT_DATE,
OrderDate) AS DaysSinceOrder
FROM Orders;
```

This query calculates the number of days since each order, highlighting older orders that may need attention.

Step 2: Estimating Delivery Dates Based on Order Date

To improve delivery tracking, the business estimates delivery dates as 5 days after the order date.

```sql
SELECT OrderID, OrderDate, DATE_ADD(OrderDate,
INTERVAL 5 DAY) AS EstimatedDeliveryDate
FROM Orders;
```

This query calculates a 5-day delivery timeline from each order date, providing estimated delivery dates.

Step 3: Identifying Inactive Customers

For retention efforts, the business wants to find customers who haven't placed an order in the last year.

```sql
SELECT CustomerID, LastOrderDate
FROM Customers
WHERE LastOrderDate < DATE_SUB(CURRENT_DATE, INTERVAL
1 YEAR);
```

This query identifies customers who haven't ordered in over a year, allowing the business to create targeted campaigns to re-engage these customers.

Section 11.6: Practice Exercises with Date Manipulation

Now, let's try some exercises to practice date and time manipulation.

Exercise 1: Calculate Customer Loyalty Duration

1. **Goal**: Calculate the number of days each customer has been with the company since their SignupDate.
2. **Expected Output**: A list showing each customer's CustomerID and the number of days since they signed up.
3. **Solution**:

   ```sql
   ```

```
SELECT CustomerID, SignupDate,
DATEDIFF(CURRENT_DATE, SignupDate) AS
DaysWithCompany
FROM Customers;
```

Exercise 2: Identify Orders from Last Month

1. **Goal**: Retrieve all orders placed in the previous month.
2. **Expected Output**: A list of orders with their `OrderID`, `OrderDate`, and `Amount`.
3. **Solution**:

```
sql
SELECT OrderID, OrderDate, Amount
FROM Orders
WHERE OrderDate BETWEEN DATE_SUB(CURRENT_DATE,
INTERVAL 1 MONTH) AND CURRENT_DATE;
```

Exercise 3: Find Products Nearing Expiration

1. **Goal**: Retrieve products whose `ExpirationDate` is within the next 30 days.
2. **Expected Output**: A list of `ProductID`s and `ExpirationDate`s for items expiring soon.
3. **Solution**:

```
sql
SELECT ProductID, ProductName, ExpirationDate
FROM Products
WHERE ExpirationDate BETWEEN CURRENT_DATE AND
DATE_ADD(CURRENT_DATE, INTERVAL 30 DAY);
```

Exercise 4: Format Order Dates for Reporting

1. **Goal**: Format order dates as `YYYY/MM/DD` for a report.
2. **Expected Output**: A list showing each `OrderID` and the formatted `OrderDate`.
3. **Solution**:

```sql
SELECT OrderID, DATE_FORMAT(OrderDate,
'%Y/%m/%d') AS FormattedOrderDate
FROM Orders;
```

Section 11.7: Common Mistakes and Best Practices with Date and Time Functions

Here are some best practices to keep in mind when working with dates and times in SQL:

1. **Use Standardized Date Formats**: Store dates in a standard format (YYYY-MM-DD), which SQL can process more reliably. Avoid using custom formats for storage.

2. **Be Cautious with Time Zones**: If working with international data, be mindful of time zones. Some SQL databases have functions for handling time zones if needed.

3. **Use DATE_FORMAT for Readable Output**: Use DATE_FORMAT to display dates in user-friendly formats, especially in reports or exports.

4. **Double-Check Date Intervals**: When using DATE_ADD and DATE_SUB, verify the interval (e.g., DAY, MONTH, YEAR) to ensure it aligns with your calculations.

5. **Test DATEDIFF with Null Values**: If your data has NULL dates, make sure to handle these appropriately when using DATEDIFF, as comparisons with NULL may lead to unexpected results.

Section 11.8: Summary and What's Next

In this chapter, you learned how to work with dates and times in SQL using functions like `CURRENT_DATE`, `DATE_ADD`, `DATE_SUB`, `DATEDIFF`, and `DATE_FORMAT`. We covered practical applications like tracking order timelines, estimating delivery dates, and identifying inactive customers, as well as practice exercises to build your skills.

In the next chapter, we'll explore how to create and use views, which allow you to simplify complex queries and present data in a customized way. Views can be incredibly useful for building reports and organizing data for specific use cases.

Great job on mastering date and time manipulation! Let's continue with Chapter 12 and learn more about views.

CHAPTER 12: CREATING AND USING VIEWS

Welcome to Chapter 12! In this chapter, we'll explore SQL views, a powerful feature that enables you to simplify data access, improve security, and create customized data representations for different users. Views are especially useful for non-technical users who need specific data insights without directly interacting with complex tables. By the end of this chapter, you'll understand the benefits of views, how to create and use them, and how they can make data management more efficient and secure.

Section 12.1: What is a View?

A **view** is a virtual table in SQL that is defined by a query. It doesn't store data itself but displays results based on a SELECT query on one or more tables. Views allow you to create customized data representations that meet specific requirements, such as simplified tables or summarized data, without altering the underlying tables.

For example, if you have an `Orders` table with numerous columns, you can create a view that only displays essential fields, such as `OrderID`, `CustomerID`, `OrderDate`, and `Amount`, making it easier for users to work with just the data they need.

Section 12.2: Benefits of Views for Data Abstraction and Security

Views offer several benefits, particularly for data abstraction and security:

1. **Data Abstraction**: Views allow you to create simplified versions of complex tables, displaying only the necessary fields for a specific task. This makes it easier for users to access relevant data without needing to understand the full database structure.

2. **Security**: By using views, you can control data access by granting permissions only to specific columns or rows in a table. This is especially useful when you want certain users to view specific data without giving them access to sensitive information.

3. **Simplified Queries**: Views can encapsulate complex queries, making it easier to reuse those queries and simplify report generation or other data retrieval tasks.

4. **Consistent Data Representation**: Views ensure that data remains consistent across different parts of the organization. For example, a "SalesReport" view will provide the same information to different departments, helping avoid discrepancies.

Section 12.3: Creating a View

Creating a view is straightforward. You define a SELECT query within the view, specifying the columns and tables you want to include.

The basic syntax for creating a view is:

```sql
CREATE VIEW view_name AS
SELECT column1, column2, ...
FROM table_name
WHERE condition;
```

- **view_name**: The name of the view you're creating.
- **SELECT query**: Defines the columns and conditions for the view, which will display results based on this query.

Example: Creating a "CustomerOrders" view to display recent orders for each customer.

```sql
Copy code
CREATE VIEW CustomerOrders AS
SELECT Customers.CustomerID, Customers.Name,
Orders.OrderID, Orders.OrderDate, Orders.Amount
FROM Customers
JOIN Orders ON Customers.CustomerID =
Orders.CustomerID
WHERE Orders.OrderDate >= DATE_SUB(CURRENT_DATE,
INTERVAL 1 MONTH);
```

In this example, the view CustomerOrders includes information about recent orders (within the last month) for each customer, simplifying data access for users who need quick order insights.

ection 12.4: Using Views for Report Generation

Views can make report generation simpler and more efficient, especially for non-technical users who may find direct SQL querying challenging. With a view, users can retrieve the data they need by querying the view instead of writing complex queries.

Example: Generating a Monthly Sales Report

Imagine a retail business that needs a monthly sales report showing each customer's total spending. This report requires data from both Customers and Orders tables. You can create a view called MonthlySalesReport to encapsulate the query logic and simplify reporting.

```sql
Copy code
CREATE VIEW MonthlySalesReport AS
SELECT Customers.CustomerID, Customers.Name,
SUM(Orders.Amount) AS TotalSpent,
DATE_FORMAT(Orders.OrderDate, '%Y-%m') AS Month
FROM Customers
JOIN Orders ON Customers.CustomerID =
Orders.CustomerID
GROUP BY Customers.CustomerID, Month;
```

Now, whenever someone needs a monthly sales report, they can query MonthlySalesReport without dealing with complex JOIN and GROUP BY operations.

```sql
Copy code
SELECT * FROM MonthlySalesReport;
```

The view automatically calculates each customer's monthly spending, making it easy for non-technical users to retrieve sales insights.

Section 12.5: Managing Views – Updating and Dropping Views

After creating a view, you may need to update or remove it as requirements change.

Updating a View

To modify an existing view, use the `CREATE OR REPLACE VIEW` statement. This allows you to redefine the view without having to drop and recreate it.

Example: Adding a new column to the `CustomerOrders` view.

```sql
Copy code
CREATE OR REPLACE VIEW CustomerOrders AS
SELECT Customers.CustomerID, Customers.Name,
Orders.OrderID, Orders.OrderDate, Orders.Amount,
Orders.Status
FROM Customers
JOIN Orders ON Customers.CustomerID =
Orders.CustomerID
WHERE Orders.OrderDate >= DATE_SUB(CURRENT_DATE,
INTERVAL 1 MONTH);
```

In this updated view, we've added the `Status` column from the `Orders` table.

Dropping a View

If a view is no longer needed, you can remove it using the `DROP VIEW` command.

```sql
Copy code
DROP VIEW view_name;
```

Example:

```sql
Copy code
DROP VIEW CustomerOrders;
```

This command removes the `CustomerOrders` view from the database. Be cautious with `DROP VIEW` as this action cannot be undone.

Section 12.6: Real-World Use Case – Simplifying Report Generation for Non-Technical Users

Let's look at a scenario where a view can simplify data access for non-technical users. Suppose a company's sales team wants to track their monthly customer sales performance but isn't familiar with SQL. The database contains Customers, Orders, and Products tables, each with many columns. Creating a view that summarizes monthly customer sales makes it easier for the team to retrieve the data they need.

Step 1: Create a View for Monthly Sales Summary

This view summarizes monthly sales for each customer, including the number of orders and total amount spent.

```sql
Copy code
CREATE VIEW MonthlyCustomerSales AS
SELECT Customers.CustomerID, Customers.Name,
COUNT(Orders.OrderID) AS OrderCount,
SUM(Orders.Amount) AS TotalSpent,
DATE_FORMAT(Orders.OrderDate, '%Y-%m') AS Month
FROM Customers
JOIN Orders ON Customers.CustomerID =
Orders.CustomerID
GROUP BY Customers.CustomerID, Month;
```

Step 2: Simplified Query for the Sales Team

Once the view is created, the sales team can easily retrieve monthly sales information without complex SQL knowledge.

```sql
Copy code
SELECT * FROM MonthlyCustomerSales;
```

This query provides a report with each customer's total orders and spending for each month, allowing the sales team to track performance easily.

Section 12.7: Practice Exercises on Creating and Managing Views

Let's reinforce your understanding of views with some practical exercises.

Exercise 1: Create a ProductInventory View

1. **Goal**: Create a view that shows each product's name, category, and stock level from the `Products` table.
2. **Expected Output**: A simplified view showing product details for inventory tracking.
3. **Solution**:

```sql
Copy code
CREATE VIEW ProductInventory AS
SELECT ProductID, ProductName, Category,
Quantity
FROM Products;
```

Exercise 2: Create a Quarterly Sales Summary View

1. **Goal**: Create a view that summarizes sales by quarter, showing each customer's total orders and total spending per quarter.
2. **Expected Output**: A view displaying quarterly sales data for each customer.
3. **Solution**:

```sql
Copy code
CREATE VIEW QuarterlySalesSummary AS
```

```sql
SELECT Customers.CustomerID, Customers.Name,
SUM(Orders.Amount) AS TotalSpent,
QUARTER(Orders.OrderDate) AS Quarter,
YEAR(Orders.OrderDate) AS Year
FROM Customers
JOIN Orders ON Customers.CustomerID =
Orders.CustomerID
GROUP BY Customers.CustomerID, Year, Quarter;
```

Exercise 3: Modify an Existing View

1. **Goal**: Add the `Email` column to the
   `MonthlyCustomerSales` view to show customer contact
   information.
2. **Solution**:

```sql
sql
Copy code
CREATE OR REPLACE VIEW MonthlyCustomerSales AS
SELECT Customers.CustomerID, Customers.Name,
Customers.Email, COUNT(Orders.OrderID) AS
OrderCount, SUM(Orders.Amount) AS TotalSpent,
DATE_FORMAT(Orders.OrderDate, '%Y-%m') AS Month
FROM Customers
JOIN Orders ON Customers.CustomerID =
Orders.CustomerID
GROUP BY Customers.CustomerID, Month;
```

Exercise 4: Drop an Unused View

1. **Goal**: Remove the `ProductInventory` view if it's no
   longer needed.
2. **Solution**:

```sql
sql
Copy code
DROP VIEW ProductInventory;
```

Section 12.8: Common Mistakes and Best Practices with Views

Here are some best practices to keep in mind when working with views:

1. **Name Views Clearly**: Use descriptive names that indicate the view's purpose (e.g., MonthlySalesReport). This makes it easier for other users to understand the view's content.

2. **Limit Columns to Essentials**: Include only the columns needed for specific use cases. Views with too many columns can become cluttered and defeat the purpose of data abstraction.

3. **Avoid Complex Joins in Views if Possible**: While views support complex joins, simpler queries within views are generally more efficient and easier to maintain. Consider breaking down complex requirements into multiple views.

4. **Use CREATE OR REPLACE to Update Views**: Use CREATE OR REPLACE to update views without needing to drop and recreate them. This approach is safer and reduces the risk of accidental deletion.

5. **Grant View Permissions Carefully**: Grant permissions to views as needed. Users with access to a view don't necessarily need access to the underlying tables, which enhances data security.

Section 12.9: Summary and What's Next

In this chapter, you learned about SQL views, their benefits, and how to use them to simplify data access and improve security. You explored how to create views, manage them, and apply them in practical scenarios such as report generation for non-technical users.

In the next chapter, we'll dive into stored procedures and functions, which allow you to automate database operations and reuse code, further enhancing your SQL toolkit.

CHAPTER 13: STORED PROCEDURES AND FUNCTIONS

Welcome to Chapter 13! In this chapter, we'll explore **stored procedures** and **user-defined functions (UDFs)**, two powerful tools in SQL that enable you to automate tasks, make calculations, and reuse code. Stored procedures and functions allow you to encapsulate complex SQL operations into single commands, boosting efficiency and ensuring consistency across tasks. By the end of this chapter, you'll understand how to create, use, and apply stored procedures and functions in practical scenarios.

Section 13.1: What are Stored Procedures and Functions?

Stored Procedures and **User-Defined Functions (UDFs)** are blocks of SQL code saved in the database. They perform specific tasks, such as automating data updates or performing calculations, and can be reused as needed.

- **Stored Procedure**: A stored procedure is a set of SQL statements that performs a specific task. It can accept input parameters, execute commands, and return results or messages. Stored procedures are versatile and can be used to automate repetitive tasks or perform actions that involve multiple steps.

- **User-Defined Function (UDF)**: A UDF performs a calculation and returns a single value or table of values.

Unlike stored procedures, functions are generally used in SELECT queries for calculations or transformations. UDFs can simplify queries by encapsulating logic in a reusable way.

Section 13.2: Benefits of Using Stored Procedures and Functions
Stored procedures and functions provide several benefits:

1. **Automation**: Stored procedures can automate repetitive tasks, such as daily data updates, reporting, or batch processing, improving efficiency.
2. **Code Reusability**: With stored procedures and UDFs, you can create reusable code that can be called as needed, reducing duplication.
3. **Improved Performance**: Stored procedures are precompiled, meaning they can execute more quickly than standard SQL queries, especially in complex operations.
4. **Enhanced Security**: By granting users access to stored procedures or functions rather than underlying tables, you can better control data access and maintain security.
5. **Consistent Calculations**: UDFs ensure that calculations are consistent, avoiding discrepancies across multiple queries.

Section 13.3: Creating Stored Procedures
Stored procedures are defined using the CREATE PROCEDURE statement, which includes the procedure name, any input parameters,

and the body of the procedure containing the SQL statements. Here's the basic syntax:

```sql
Copy code
CREATE PROCEDURE procedure_name (parameter_list)
BEGIN
    -- SQL statements
END;
```

- **procedure_name**: The name of the stored procedure.

- **parameter_list**: Optional parameters that the procedure accepts.

- **SQL statements**: The SQL commands to execute within the procedure.

Example: Creating a Procedure to Update Inventory Levels

Suppose a retail business needs to automate inventory updates by deducting quantities from the inventory table after each sale. Here's how a stored procedure can accomplish this:

```sql
Copy code
CREATE PROCEDURE UpdateInventory (IN product_id INT,
IN quantity_sold INT)
BEGIN
    UPDATE Inventory
    SET Quantity = Quantity - quantity_sold
    WHERE ProductID = product_id;
END;
```

- **IN**: Specifies that `product_id` and `quantity_sold` are input parameters.

- **UPDATE Inventory**: The procedure reduces the `Quantity` by `quantity_sold` for the specified `product_id`.

Calling the Stored Procedure

To execute the procedure, use the `CALL` statement:

```sql
CALL UpdateInventory(101, 5);
```
This command reduces the quantity of product with `ProductID` 101 by 5.

Section 13.4: Creating User-Defined Functions (UDFs)

UDFs are defined using the `CREATE FUNCTION` statement. Functions return a single value and are often used within `SELECT` queries for calculations or transformations. Here's the basic syntax:

```sql
CREATE FUNCTION function_name (parameter_list)
RETURNS data_type
BEGIN
    -- SQL statements
    RETURN value;
END;
```

- **function_name**: The name of the function.
- **parameter_list**: Optional input parameters for the function.
- **RETURNS**: Specifies the data type of the value the function returns.
- **RETURN**: Specifies the value the function returns.

Example: Creating a Function to Calculate Discounted Price**

Suppose a business wants to calculate a discounted price for each product based on a discount percentage. Here's how a UDF can accomplish this:

```sql
CREATE FUNCTION CalculateDiscountedPrice
(original_price DECIMAL(10, 2), discount_rate
DECIMAL(5, 2))
RETURNS DECIMAL(10, 2)
BEGIN
    DECLARE discounted_price DECIMAL(10, 2);
    SET discounted_price = original_price -
(original_price * discount_rate / 100);
    RETURN discounted_price;
END;
```

This function takes two parameters—original_price and discount_rate—and returns the price after applying the discount.

Using the Function in a Query

You can use the CalculateDiscountedPrice function within a SELECT query to calculate the discounted price of each product.

```sql
SELECT ProductName, Price,
CalculateDiscountedPrice(Price, 10) AS
DiscountedPrice
FROM Products;
```

This query calculates a 10% discounted price for each product, displaying it in a new column.

Section 13.5: Real-World Example – Automating Data Updates and Calculations

Stored procedures and functions can streamline processes for a business. Let's explore an example where a retail business uses these tools to automate inventory updates and calculate discounts.

Example: Automating Daily Inventory Updates

The business wants to automate a daily update that reduces inventory levels based on recent sales data stored in the Sales table. The stored procedure, UpdateDailyInventory, will deduct quantities sold from the Inventory table for each product sold.

1. **Creating the Procedure**:

```sql
CREATE PROCEDURE UpdateDailyInventory ()
BEGIN
    DECLARE product_id INT;
    DECLARE quantity_sold INT;

    DECLARE done INT DEFAULT 0;
    DECLARE sales_cursor CURSOR FOR SELECT
ProductID, Quantity FROM Sales;
    DECLARE CONTINUE HANDLER FOR NOT FOUND SET
done = 1;

    OPEN sales_cursor;

    sales_loop: LOOP
        FETCH sales_cursor INTO product_id,
quantity_sold;
        IF done = 1 THEN
            LEAVE sales_loop;
        END IF;
        CALL UpdateInventory(product_id,
quantity_sold);
    END LOOP;

    CLOSE sales_cursor;
END;
```

This procedure:

- o Uses a cursor to loop through each sale in the Sales table.

- o **Calls the** UpdateInventory **procedure for each product to reduce the inventory.**

2. **Executing the Procedure**:

To update inventory levels, the business simply runs:

```sql
CALL UpdateDailyInventory();
```

Example: Calculating and Displaying Discounted Prices

The business wants to display discounted prices to customers based on different discount percentages.

1. **Using the Function in a Query**:

```sql
SELECT ProductName, Price,
CalculateDiscountedPrice(Price, 15) AS
DiscountedPrice
FROM Products;
```

This query calculates a 15% discount for each product and displays the discounted price alongside the original price.

Section 13.6: Practical Exercises to Boost Efficiency with Reusable Code

Try these exercises to practice creating and using stored procedures and functions.

Exercise 1: Create a Procedure for Bulk Price Updates

1. **Goal**: Write a stored procedure called UpdatePrices that applies a percentage increase to all products in the Products table.

2. **Solution**:

```sql
CREATE PROCEDURE UpdatePrices (IN increase_rate
DECIMAL(5, 2))
BEGIN
    UPDATE Products
    SET Price = Price + (Price * increase_rate
/ 100);
END;
```

This procedure increases the price of each product by a specified percentage.

Exercise 2: Create a Function to Calculate Sales Tax

1. **Goal**: Write a function called CalculateSalesTax that calculates sales tax based on a product price and a tax rate.
2. **Solution**:

```sql
CREATE FUNCTION CalculateSalesTax (price
DECIMAL(10, 2), tax_rate DECIMAL(5, 2))
RETURNS DECIMAL(10, 2)
BEGIN
    RETURN price * tax_rate / 100;
END;
```

This function calculates the tax amount based on the product price and a given tax rate.

Exercise 3: Create a Procedure to Archive Old Orders

1. **Goal**: Write a stored procedure that moves orders older than 1 year from the Orders table to an ArchivedOrders table.
2. **Solution**:

```sql
CREATE PROCEDURE ArchiveOldOrders ()
```

```
BEGIN
    INSERT INTO ArchivedOrders (OrderID,
CustomerID, OrderDate, Amount)
    SELECT OrderID, CustomerID, OrderDate,
Amount
    FROM Orders
    WHERE OrderDate < DATE_SUB(CURRENT_DATE,
INTERVAL 1 YEAR);

    DELETE FROM Orders
    WHERE OrderDate < DATE_SUB(CURRENT_DATE,
INTERVAL 1 YEAR);
END;
```

This procedure transfers old orders to the `ArchivedOrders`
table and deletes them from the `Orders` table.

Section 13.7: Common Mistakes and Best Practices with Stored Procedures and Functions

Here are some tips to keep in mind when working with stored procedures and functions:

1. **Use Descriptive Names**: Name your procedures and functions based on their purpose (e.g., CalculateDiscountedPrice). This makes them easier to understand and reuse.

2. **Limit Side Effects in Functions**: Functions should generally avoid modifying data, as they're designed for calculations and transformations. Use procedures for data updates.

3. **Set Permissions Carefully**: Restrict access to stored procedures and functions as needed, particularly if they modify sensitive data.

4. **Handle NULLs and Default Values**: Always consider how your procedure or function will handle NULL values. Define default values for input parameters when appropriate.

5. **Test with Sample Data**: Before deploying stored procedures and functions in production, test them thoroughly to ensure they perform as expected and handle edge cases.

Section 13.8: Summary and What's Next

In this chapter, you learned about stored procedures and functions, how they improve efficiency, and how to create reusable code for automating tasks and calculations. You explored practical applications, such as updating inventory levels and calculating discounts, and completed exercises to reinforce your understanding.

In the next chapter, we'll look at error handling and debugging in SQL, so you'll be prepared to troubleshoot issues and maintain robust code as you work with stored procedures and functions.

Great job on mastering stored procedures and functions—let's move on to Chapter 14!

CHAPTER 14: TRANSACTIONS AND DATA INTEGRITY

Welcome to Chapter 14! In this chapter, we'll cover **transactions** and **data integrity**, essential concepts for ensuring that SQL operations are consistent, reliable, and error-free. Transactions allow you to bundle multiple SQL statements into a single unit of work, ensuring data remains consistent even if part of the process fails. You'll learn about **ACID properties**—the fundamental principles that support reliable transactions—and explore a real-world scenario in e-commerce for consistent order processing. By the end of this chapter, you'll understand how to use transactions to maintain data integrity and perform practice exercises with transactions and rollbacks.

Section 14.1: Importance of Transactions and ACID Properties

A **transaction** is a series of SQL operations that are executed as a single unit. Transactions are crucial for data integrity because they ensure that all operations are completed successfully, or none are applied, thereby keeping the database in a consistent state.

The **ACID properties** define the principles of reliable transactions. ACID stands for:

1. **Atomicity**: Ensures that all operations within a transaction are completed successfully, or none are applied. If any operation fails, the entire transaction is rolled back.

2. **Consistency**: Ensures that a transaction transforms the database from one valid state to another, maintaining database rules, constraints, and integrity.

3. **Isolation**: Guarantees that transactions are executed independently of one another. Changes made in a transaction aren't visible to other transactions until the transaction is complete.

4. **Durability**: Ensures that once a transaction is committed, the changes are permanent, even if there's a system failure.

Together, these properties help maintain data integrity, especially in environments with multiple users and complex operations.

Section 14.2: Using Transactions in SQL

SQL transactions are typically managed with the following commands:

- **BEGIN** or **START TRANSACTION**: Starts a new transaction.
- **COMMIT**: Saves all changes made during the transaction, making them permanent.
- **ROLLBACK**: Undoes all changes made during the transaction, returning the database to its previous state.

Basic Syntax for Transactions

```sql
BEGIN;
-- SQL operations
```

```
COMMIT;
```
or

```
sql
```

```
START TRANSACTION;
-- SQL operations
ROLLBACK;
```

Using COMMIT applies the changes made within the transaction, while ROLLBACK cancels them if something goes wrong.

Section 14.3: Real-World Application – Ensuring Consistent Order Processing in E-Commerce

Let's explore a real-world scenario where transactions are essential. Imagine an e-commerce platform where customers place orders. For each order, the database needs to update inventory levels, record the order, and process payment. All of these actions should happen as a single transaction to ensure consistency. If any part of the transaction fails—such as an issue with payment—none of the updates should be applied.

Example: Processing an Order with Transactions

Suppose we have the following tables:

- **Inventory**: Stores product information and stock levels.
- **Orders**: Stores customer orders.
- **Payments**: Records payment transactions.

The transaction steps for processing an order would be:

1. Decrease the product quantity in the Inventory table.

2. Insert the new order into the `Orders` **table.**
3. Record the payment in the `Payments` **table.**

Here's how this could be implemented with a transaction:

```sql
sql

START TRANSACTION;

-- Step 1: Update inventory levels
UPDATE Inventory
SET Quantity = Quantity - 1
WHERE ProductID = 101;

-- Step 2: Insert the order
INSERT INTO Orders (OrderID, CustomerID, ProductID,
OrderDate, Quantity)
VALUES (1001, 2001, 101, CURRENT_DATE, 1);

-- Step 3: Record the payment
INSERT INTO Payments (PaymentID, OrderID, Amount,
PaymentDate)
VALUES (3001, 1001, 50.00, CURRENT_DATE);

-- Commit the transaction if all steps are successful
COMMIT;
```

If any of these steps fail (for instance, if there's insufficient stock in the `Inventory` table), the transaction can be rolled back to prevent incomplete updates.

```sql
sql
ROLLBACK;
```

In this example, either all three steps are applied, or none, maintaining data integrity.

Section 14.4: Practice Exercises with Transactions and Rollbacks

Let's practice using transactions in various scenarios to reinforce your understanding.

Exercise 1: Adding a New Customer and Initializing Their Account Balance

1. **Goal**: Write a transaction to add a new customer and create an associated account with a starting balance.
2. **Expected Output**: A new customer and account record, but only if both actions succeed.
3. **Solution**:

```sql
START TRANSACTION;

-- Step 1: Add the new customer
INSERT INTO Customers (CustomerID, Name, Email,
SignupDate)
VALUES (3001, 'Alex Johnson',
'alex.j@example.com', CURRENT_DATE);

-- Step 2: Initialize the account balance
INSERT INTO Accounts (CustomerID, Balance)
VALUES (3001, 100.00);

-- Commit if both steps are successful
COMMIT;
```

If an error occurs in either step, roll back the transaction:

```sql
ROLLBACK;
```

Exercise 2: Transferring Funds Between Two Accounts

1. **Goal**: Write a transaction to transfer funds between two accounts. The transfer should only proceed if both accounts have sufficient balances.

2. **Expected Output**: Both accounts are updated only if funds are sufficient.

3. **Solution**:

sql

```sql
START TRANSACTION;

-- Step 1: Deduct from sender's account
UPDATE Accounts
SET Balance = Balance - 50
WHERE CustomerID = 3001 AND Balance >= 50;

-- Step 2: Add to recipient's account
UPDATE Accounts
SET Balance = Balance + 50
WHERE CustomerID = 3002;

-- Commit if both steps are successful
COMMIT;
```

If the sender's account balance is insufficient, roll back the transaction:

sql
```sql
ROLLBACK;
```

Exercise 3: Cancelling an Order and Restoring Inventory

1. **Goal**: Write a transaction to cancel an order and restore the product's inventory.
2. **Expected Output**: The order is deleted and inventory updated, or neither action takes effect.
3. **Solution**:

```sql
sql
START TRANSACTION;

-- Step 1: Delete the order
DELETE FROM Orders
WHERE OrderID = 1001;

-- Step 2: Restore inventory level
UPDATE Inventory
```

```
SET Quantity = Quantity + 1
WHERE ProductID = 101;

-- Commit if both steps are successful
COMMIT;
```
If there's an issue with either step, roll back the transaction:

```sql
ROLLBACK;
```

Section 14.5: Best Practices for Using Transactions

Transactions are powerful, but to use them effectively, consider these best practices:

1. **Keep Transactions Short**: Limit the number of statements in a transaction to avoid locking issues and improve performance. Shorter transactions reduce the risk of deadlocks and improve database response times.

2. **Use Explicit Rollbacks for Error Handling**: Use ROLLBACK to undo changes if any part of a transaction fails. This keeps the database in a consistent state.

3. **Handle Errors Appropriately**: Implement error-handling mechanisms to catch issues within a transaction. In many SQL implementations, you can use conditions or error-handling statements for this.

4. **Use Savepoints in Complex Transactions**: If a transaction has multiple stages, use savepoints to mark points within the transaction. This way, you can roll back to specific stages instead of canceling the entire transaction.

5. **Avoid User Interaction During Transactions**: Avoid prompting users or waiting for external input during a transaction. Keeping transactions open for extended periods can lock rows or tables, impacting other operations.

Section 14.6: Summary and What's Next

In this chapter, you learned about transactions and the ACID properties that ensure data integrity. You practiced using BEGIN, COMMIT, and ROLLBACK commands to maintain consistent data states during operations, particularly in scenarios like e-commerce order processing. Understanding transactions is essential for building reliable, scalable applications that involve complex data updates.

In the next chapter, we'll cover **SQL triggers**—another powerful feature that allows you to automate responses to database events. Triggers work well with transactions, and together, they form a strong foundation for managing database workflows effectively.

CHAPTER 15: INDEXING FOR PERFORMANCE OPTIMIZATION

Welcome to Chapter 15! In this chapter, we'll cover **indexing**, an essential technique for optimizing SQL performance. Indexes improve query speed by allowing the database to locate rows quickly without scanning every row in a table. However, indexes come with trade-offs, such as increased storage and slower write operations. By the end of this chapter, you'll understand the benefits and trade-offs of indexing, see how it applies to real-world scenarios, and learn best practices for creating and maintaining indexes.

Section 15.1: What is an Index?

An **index** is a data structure that SQL uses to speed up the retrieval of rows based on specific columns. Indexes work like a book's table of contents, enabling the database to locate data efficiently without searching every row. When you create an index on a column, SQL builds a sorted structure that allows for faster lookup of data in that column.

Indexes are typically used on columns that are frequently involved in:

- **WHERE clauses**: Filtering queries to find specific values.
- **JOIN operations**: Matching rows between tables.
- **ORDER BY** and **GROUP BY** clauses: Sorting or grouping data for reporting.

While indexes significantly improve read performance, they can slow down write operations (inserts, updates, deletes) because the database must maintain the index structure each time the data changes.

Section 15.2: Benefits and Trade-Offs of Using Indexes

Indexes provide notable advantages, but they also come with trade-offs:

Benefits of Indexes

1. **Faster Query Performance**: Indexes speed up data retrieval, especially for large datasets, by allowing SQL to quickly locate rows without scanning the entire table.
2. **Efficient Sorting and Grouping**: Indexes improve the performance of ORDER BY and GROUP BY operations by organizing data in a sorted structure, making it easier to group or rank results.
3. **Improved JOIN Performance**: Indexes on foreign keys in related tables improve the speed of JOIN operations by allowing SQL to match rows efficiently.

Trade-Offs of Indexes

1. **Increased Storage Requirements**: Each index requires additional disk space. Large datasets with multiple indexes can result in substantial storage overhead.
2. **Slower Write Operations**: Every INSERT, UPDATE, or DELETE operation on a table with indexes requires additional processing to keep the index structure up-to-date, which can slow down write operations.
3. **Maintenance Overhead**: Indexes require periodic maintenance to ensure they remain effective. For instance,

outdated indexes may become fragmented, requiring optimization.

In general, indexes should be used thoughtfully on columns that are frequently queried. Over-indexing can lead to diminishing returns by slowing down write operations and increasing storage costs.

Section 15.3: Real-World Example – Speeding Up Search Queries on Large Customer Datasets

Let's look at a practical scenario where indexing can dramatically improve performance. Imagine an e-commerce platform with a `Customers` table containing millions of records. Queries that filter customers by email, location, or signup date could become slow as the dataset grows. Indexing the columns most commonly used in search queries can help reduce query times.

Example: Creating Indexes to Optimize Customer Search Queries

Suppose the `Customers` table includes the following columns:

- **CustomerID** (Primary Key)
- **Name**
- **Email**
- **SignupDate**
- **City**

The database frequently handles queries like:

1. Finding customers by email.

2. Searching customers by city.
3. Retrieving recent signups.

By creating indexes on the Email, City, and SignupDate columns, you can improve the performance of these queries.

```sql
Copy code
-- Creating an index on the Email column
CREATE INDEX idx_email ON Customers (Email);

-- Creating an index on the City column
CREATE INDEX idx_city ON Customers (City);

-- Creating an index on the SignupDate column
CREATE INDEX idx_signup_date ON Customers (SignupDate);
```

With these indexes, SQL can quickly find customers based on email, city, or signup date without scanning the entire Customers table. This can make a significant difference in performance for a large dataset.

Example Query Performance Before and After Indexing

Let's compare a query for retrieving a customer by email, with and without indexing.

Without Index:

```sql
Copy code
SELECT * FROM Customers WHERE Email = 'john.doe@example.com';
```

In a large table without an index on Email, SQL performs a full table scan to find matching records, which can be time-consuming.

With Index:

```sql
Copy code
SELECT * FROM Customers WHERE Email =
'john.doe@example.com';
```

With an index on `Email`, SQL can locate the matching row quickly, bypassing rows that don't match. This index dramatically reduces the time needed for this query.

Section 15.4: Guidelines for Creating and Maintaining Indexes

Indexes can greatly enhance performance if used correctly. Here are best practices for creating and maintaining indexes:

1. **Index Frequently Queried Columns**: Focus on columns used in WHERE clauses, joins, and sorting operations. Avoid indexing columns that are rarely used in queries, as the index overhead may not justify the benefit.

2. **Avoid Over-Indexing**: Adding too many indexes can lead to performance issues with write operations and increased storage requirements. Only index columns that provide significant query performance gains.

3. **Use Composite Indexes for Multi-Column Searches**: When queries filter by multiple columns, consider using a composite (multi-column) index to improve performance. For example, an index on both City and SignupDate is useful if a query searches by city and filters by date.

```sql
```

```
Copy code
CREATE INDEX idx_city_signup_date ON Customers
(City, SignupDate);
```

4. **Consider Index Selectivity**: Selectivity refers to the uniqueness of values in a column. Indexing columns with high selectivity (e.g., Email or CustomerID) is more effective than indexing columns with low selectivity (e.g., Country), as it provides a more direct filter.

5. **Monitor and Maintain Indexes**: Over time, indexes can become fragmented, which may slow down query performance. Regularly monitor and maintain indexes by rebuilding or reorganizing them, especially on large tables with frequent updates.

6. **Primary and Foreign Keys**: Primary keys are indexed automatically, so no additional index is required. For foreign keys, adding an index can improve JOIN performance, particularly when working with large datasets.

7. **Avoid Indexing Columns with High Update Frequency**: Columns that frequently change, like Status or LastLogin, may not be ideal candidates for indexing. The overhead of updating the index structure each time the column value changes can impact performance.

Section 15.5: Practice Exercises with Indexing

Let's try some exercises to practice creating and evaluating indexes.

Exercise 1: Indexing a Column for Search Performance

1. **Goal**: Create an index on the Email column in the Customers table to improve search performance for queries filtering by email.

2. **Expected Output**: A faster query response time when searching by email.

3. **Solution**:

sql
CREATE INDEX idx_email ON Customers (Email);

Exercise 2: Creating a Composite Index

1. **Goal**: Create a composite index on the City and SignupDate columns in the Customers table to improve search performance for queries filtering by both city and signup date.

2. **Expected Output**: A faster query response time when filtering by both city and signup date.

3. **Solution**:

```
sql
CREATE INDEX idx_city_signup_date ON Customers
(City, SignupDate);
```

Exercise 3: Evaluating Index Trade-Offs for a Frequently Updated Column

1. **Goal**: Evaluate whether it's beneficial to index the LastLogin column, which is updated frequently.

2. **Analysis**: Because Last Login is updated each time a customer logs in, indexing this column may slow down updates. Instead, consider whether this index will significantly improve query performance for common queries, and weigh it against the update overhead.

Exercise 4: Dropping an Unused Index

1. **Goal**: Drop an index on a rarely used column (`MiddleName` in the `Customers` table) to reduce storage and update overhead.
2. **Solution**:

```sql
Copy code
DROP INDEX idx_middle_name ON Customers;
```

Section 15.6: Common Mistakes and Best Practices with Indexing

Here are some tips to avoid common mistakes with indexes:

1. **Index for Specific Query Needs**: Only create indexes based on the queries that your application frequently uses. Avoid creating indexes without considering the specific needs of your database queries.
2. **Monitor Query Performance**: Use SQL's query optimization tools (e.g., EXPLAIN in MySQL) to analyze query performance before and after indexing. This can help you understand whether an index is beneficial.

3. **Limit Indexes on Small Tables**: For small tables, indexes may not yield noticeable performance benefits. SQL can efficiently scan small tables without indexes, so the overhead may not be justified.

4. **Maintain Indexes Regularly**: Rebuild or reorganize indexes periodically, especially on tables with high update frequency. This helps reduce fragmentation and maintain performance.

5. **Consider the Order of Columns in Composite Indexes**: For multi-column indexes, arrange columns based on the query's filtering order. SQL generally benefits from indexes that match the column order used in the query conditions.

Section 15.7: Summary and What's Next

In this chapter, you learned about indexing, its benefits, and the trade-offs involved. You explored how to use indexes to optimize query performance in scenarios like searching large customer datasets, as well as best practices for creating and maintaining indexes. Effective indexing can dramatically improve SQL performance, particularly with large tables and frequent read operations.

In the next chapter, we'll cover **SQL triggers**—powerful tools that automatically respond to database events like inserts, updates, and deletes. Triggers work well with indexes, as they allow you to automate actions that maintain data integrity and improve workflow efficiency.

Great work on mastering indexing for performance optimization— let's continue to Chapter 16!

CHAPTER 16: DATABASE NORMALIZATION AND OPTIMIZATION TECHNIQUES

Welcome to Chapter 16! In this chapter, we'll explore **database normalization** and other **optimization techniques** that improve the structure, efficiency, and performance of a database. Normalization is the process of organizing data to reduce redundancy and ensure consistency, helping maintain data integrity in large databases. By the end of this chapter, you'll understand the principles of normalization (1NF, 2NF, 3NF), how and when to apply them, and how they impact real-world database design, such as structuring a product catalog for minimal redundancy.

Section 16.1: What is Database Normalization?

Database normalization is the process of organizing tables and fields in a relational database to minimize redundancy and dependency. The goal is to structure data logically, making it easier to maintain and query. Normalization typically involves splitting large tables into smaller, related tables and defining relationships between them.

Normalization progresses through **normal forms (NFs)**, with each level introducing stricter rules for table design. Here's a quick overview of the first three normal forms:

1. **First Normal Form (1NF)**: Ensures that columns contain atomic (indivisible) values and each record is unique.

2. **Second Normal Form (2NF)**: Builds on 1NF by ensuring that each non-key column depends on the entire primary key (eliminating partial dependencies).

3. **Third Normal Form (3NF)**: Builds on 2NF by ensuring that each non-key column is independent of other non-key columns, known as removing transitive dependencies.

Each normal form minimizes data redundancy, making data updates more efficient and reducing the risk of anomalies.

Section 16.2: The Normalization Process – 1NF, 2NF, and 3NF
Let's dive deeper into each normal form with examples to understand the transformation process.

First Normal Form (1NF)
In 1NF, a table must satisfy two conditions:

1. Each cell contains atomic (indivisible) values.
2. Each record (row) is unique.

Example: Assume we have a `Products` table with the following structure:

ProductID	ProductName	Categories	Price
1	Coffee	Beverages, Hot Drinks	5.99
2	Tea	Beverages, Hot Drinks	3.99

The `Categories` column contains multiple values (e.g., "Beverages, Hot Drinks"), which violates 1NF. To make this table 1NF-compliant, we need to split `Categories` into individual records, as shown below:

ProductID	ProductName	Category	Price
1	Coffee	Beverages	5.99
1	Coffee	Hot Drinks	5.99
2	Tea	Beverages	3.99
2	Tea	Hot Drinks	3.99

Now, each cell contains a single, atomic value, and the table meets 1NF requirements.

Second Normal Form (2NF)

To satisfy 2NF, the table must first be in 1NF and also meet the following condition:

- All non-key columns depend on the entire primary key, not just part of it (no partial dependencies).

Example: Suppose we have an `OrderDetails` table with a composite primary key (`OrderID`, `ProductID`) and the following structure:

OrderID	ProductID	ProductName	Quantity	Price
101	1	Coffee	2	5.99
102	2	Tea	1	3.99

Here, `ProductName` and `Price` depend only on `ProductID`, not the entire primary key (`OrderID`, `ProductID`). To resolve this, we can split `OrderDetails` into two tables:

1. **OrderDetails** (stores `OrderID`, `ProductID`, and `Quantity`):

OrderID	ProductID	Quantity
101	1	2
102	2	1

2. **Products** (stores `ProductID`, `ProductName`, and `Price`):

ProductID	ProductName	Price
1	Coffee	5.99
2	Tea	3.99

Now, each non-key column depends on the entire primary key, making both tables compliant with 2NF.

Third Normal Form (3NF)

To satisfy 3NF, the table must first be in 2NF and also meet the following condition:

- Non-key columns should not depend on other non-key columns (no transitive dependencies).

Example: Suppose we have a `Customers` table with the following structure:

CustomerID	Name	City	PostalCode
1	Alice	New York	10001
2	Bob	Chicago	60601

In this case, `PostalCode` depends on `City`, not directly on the primary key (`CustomerID`). To remove this dependency, we can create a separate `Cities` table:

1. **Customers** (stores `CustomerID`, `Name`, and `City`):

CustomerID	Name	City
1	Alice	New York
2	Bob	Chicago

2. **Cities** (stores `City` and `PostalCode`):

City	PostalCode
New York	10001
Chicago	60601

Now, each non-key column depends only on the primary key, making both tables compliant with 3NF.

Section 16.3: Real-World Example – Structuring a Product Catalog for Minimal Redundancy

Let's apply these normalization principles to a product catalog. Imagine an e-commerce platform with a catalog that includes products, categories, and suppliers.

Suppose we start with a `Products` table:

ProductID	ProductName	Category	SupplierName	SupplierPhone
1	Coffee	Beverages	Supplier A	123-456-7890
2	Tea	Beverages	Supplier A	123-456-7890
3	Laptop	Electronics	Supplier B	234-567-8901

This table contains redundant information, such as repeating `Category`, `SupplierName`, and `SupplierPhone` values. Here's how we can normalize it:

1. **1NF**: Ensure atomic values. In this case, each cell already contains a single value.
2. **2NF**: Remove partial dependencies. Since `SupplierName` and `SupplierPhone` depend on the `Supplier`, we create a separate `Suppliers` table:
   - **Products**:

ProductID	ProductName	Category	SupplierID
1	Coffee	Beverages	1
2	Tea	Beverages	1
3	Laptop	Electronics	2

   - **Suppliers**:

SupplierID	SupplierName	SupplierPhone
1	Supplier A	123-456-7890
2	Supplier B	234-567-8901

3. **3NF**: Remove transitive dependencies. Since `Category` doesn't depend on the `ProductID` directly, we can create a `Categories` table to store unique categories:
   - **Products**:

ProductID	ProductName	CategoryID	SupplierID
1	Coffee	1	1
2	Tea	1	1
3	Laptop	2	2

   - **Categories**:

CategoryID	CategoryName
1	Beverages
2	Electronics

Now, the `Products` table references `Categories` and `Suppliers`, reducing redundancy and ensuring data consistency.

Section 16.4: Exercises on Identifying and Applying Normalization Principles

Let's practice applying normalization principles to different scenarios.

Exercise 1: First Normal Form

1. **Goal**: Transform a table that violates 1NF into a 1NF-compliant structure.
2. **Table**:

OrderID	ProductName	Quantity	Price
101	Coffee, Tea	2, 3	5.99, 3.99

3. **Solution**:

OrderID	ProductName	Quantity	Price
101	Coffee	2	5.99
101	Tea	3	3.99

Exercise 2: Second Normal Form

1. **Goal**: Normalize a table to 2NF by removing partial dependencies.
2. **Table**:

OrderID	ProductID	ProductName	Quantity	Price
101	1	Coffee	2	5.99
102	2	Tea	1	3.99

3. **Solution**:
   o **OrderDetails**:

OrderID	ProductID	Quantity

158

101	1	2
102	2	1

   o **Products**:

ProductID	ProductName	Price
1	Coffee	5.99
2	Tea	3.99

Exercise 3: Third Normal Form

1. **Goal**: Normalize a table to 3NF by removing transitive dependencies.
2. **Table**:

CustomerID	Name	Address	City	PostalCode
1	Alice	123 Main	NY	10001
2	Bob	456 Maple	Chicago	60601

3. **Solution**:
   o **Customers**:

CustomerID	Name	Address	CityID
1	Alice	123 Main	1
2	Bob	456 Maple	2

   o **Cities**:

CityID	City	PostalCode
1	NY	10001
2	Chicago	60601

Section 16.5: Common Mistakes and Best Practices with Normalization

1. **Avoid Over-Normalization**: Over-normalization can lead to unnecessary complexity and additional joins, which can slow down query performance. Balance normalization with practical query performance.

2. **Analyze Query Patterns**: Consider common queries on your database. Denormalization (intentionally introducing some redundancy) can sometimes improve performance for read-heavy applications.

3. **Maintain Referential Integrity**: Use foreign keys to enforce relationships between tables and ensure data consistency.

4. **Review Indexes After Normalization**: Normalization often leads to smaller, related tables. Consider indexing foreign keys and frequently queried columns in these tables to optimize performance.

Section 16.6: Summary and What's Next

In this chapter, you learned about database normalization principles, including 1NF, 2NF, and 3NF, and how they improve data structure by reducing redundancy and maintaining consistency. You explored a real-world example of structuring a product catalog and completed exercises to reinforce normalization techniques.

In the next chapter, we'll cover **advanced query optimization techniques** to further improve database performance beyond normalization, such as indexing strategies, caching, and query restructuring.

CHAPTER 17: WORKING WITH NON-RELATIONAL DATA IN SQL

Welcome to Chapter 17! In this chapter, we'll explore how SQL databases can work with **non-relational data** using **JSON** and **XML** data types. While SQL databases are traditionally used for structured data, many support these semi-structured formats, allowing you to store and query flexible data within a relational model. By the end of this chapter, you'll know how to store, retrieve, and manipulate JSON data in SQL, using it to enrich data stored in customer profiles or similar applications.

Section 17.1: Introduction to Non-Relational Data in SQL

Non-relational data refers to data that doesn't follow a strict table structure, such as JSON or XML, which is often used for hierarchical or complex data that can vary from one record to another. Many modern SQL databases (such as MySQL, PostgreSQL, and SQL Server) support **JSON** as a native data type, allowing you to store, query, and manipulate JSON directly within SQL. This capability is especially useful for applications that need to store semi-structured data, such as customer preferences or product specifications, without requiring a fixed schema.

Section 17.2: Using JSON Data Types in SQL

JSON (JavaScript Object Notation) is a popular format for storing semi-structured data because it's flexible and easy to parse. SQL databases with JSON support allow you to store JSON objects within table columns, making it possible to handle data that doesn't conform to a rigid schema.

Defining JSON Columns in a Table

To store JSON data, define a column with the `JSON` data type (or equivalent) in your table schema.

Example: Creating a `Customers` table with a `Profile` column for storing JSON data.

```sql
Copy code
CREATE TABLE Customers (
    CustomerID INT PRIMARY KEY,
    Name VARCHAR(100),
    Profile JSON
);
```

In this example, the `Profile` column holds JSON data, which could include various details about the customer, such as preferences, social media handles, or contact information.

Inserting JSON Data

JSON data is inserted as a JSON object within a single string value.

```sql
Copy code
INSERT INTO Customers (CustomerID, Name, Profile)
VALUES (1, 'Alice', '{"email": "alice@example.com",
"preferences": {"newsletter": true, "sms": false}}');
```

In this example, the `Profile` column stores a JSON object with email and preferences for the customer. This flexibility makes it easy to add new fields in the JSON object without altering the table schema.

Section 17.3: Querying JSON Data with SQL

Most SQL databases with JSON support provide functions for accessing and manipulating JSON data. Common functions include:

- **JSON_EXTRACT()**: Retrieves data from a JSON object.
- **JSON_UNQUOTE()**: Removes the quotation marks from JSON values.
- **JSON_CONTAINS()**: Checks if a JSON object contains a specified value.
- **JSON_SET()**: Updates or adds values within a JSON object.

Example: Retrieving Data from a JSON Column

Suppose we want to retrieve the `email` field from the `Profile` column for each customer. Here's how we can do this with `JSON_EXTRACT()`.

```sql
Copy code
SELECT Name, JSON_EXTRACT(Profile, '$.email') AS
Email
FROM Customers;
```

This query extracts the `email` field from each `Profile` JSON object. The `$` symbol represents the root of the JSON object, and `$.email` specifies the path to the `email` field.

Example: Checking JSON Content with JSON_CONTAINS()**

You can use `JSON_CONTAINS()` to filter rows based on JSON values.

Example: Finding customers who have opted in for the newsletter.

```sql
```

```
Copy code
SELECT Name
FROM Customers
WHERE JSON_CONTAINS(Profile, 'true',
'$.preferences.newsletter');
```

This query checks if the `newsletter` field in the `preferences` object is set to `true`. If it is, the customer's name is returned.

Section 17.4: Real-World Application – Storing and Querying Semi-Structured Customer Profiles

Let's look at a practical scenario where JSON data can simplify customer profile management. Imagine an e-commerce platform with a `Customers` table, where the `Profile` column stores each customer's preferences, contact information, and account settings as a JSON object. By using JSON, we avoid the need to add numerous columns for each potential preference or setting.

Step 1: Storing Customer Preferences

Suppose we want to store the following profile information for a customer:

- `email`: "alice@example.com"
- `preferences`: { "newsletter": true, "sms": false }
- `social`: { "twitter": "@alice" }

We can insert this data as a JSON object in the `Profile` column.

```sql
Copy code
INSERT INTO Customers (CustomerID, Name, Profile)
VALUES (1, 'Alice', '{"email": "alice@example.com",
"preferences": {"newsletter": true, "sms": false},
"social": {"twitter": "@alice"}}');
```

Step 2: Querying Customer Preferences

Now let's retrieve all customers who have opted in for SMS notifications. Since preferences are stored as JSON, we can easily filter by the `sms` preference.

```sql
Copy code
SELECT Name, JSON_EXTRACT(Profile, '$.email') AS
Email
FROM Customers
WHERE JSON_EXTRACT(Profile, '$.preferences.sms') =
'true';
```

This query returns customers with `sms` notifications set to `true`.

Step 3: Updating JSON Data

Suppose we want to update a customer's social media handle. Using `JSON_SET()`, we can modify the JSON data directly.

```sql
Copy code
UPDATE Customers
SET Profile = JSON_SET(Profile, '$.social.twitter',
'@alice_updated')
WHERE CustomerID = 1;
```

This query updates Alice's Twitter handle in the `Profile` JSON object.

Section 17.5: Practical Exercises with JSON Functions

Try these exercises to practice working with JSON data in SQL.

Exercise 1: Extracting Nested JSON Data

1. **Goal**: Retrieve the `sms` preference for each customer.
2. **Expected Output**: A list of customers with their `sms` notification preference.

3. **Solution**:

```sql
Copy code
SELECT Name, JSON_EXTRACT(Profile,
'$.preferences.sms') AS SMS_Preference
FROM Customers;
```

Exercise 2: Filtering by JSON Content

1. **Goal**: Find customers who have a Twitter handle listed in their Profile.
2. **Expected Output**: A list of customers with a Twitter handle.
3. **Solution**:

```sql
SELECT Name
FROM Customers
WHERE JSON_EXTRACT(Profile, '$.social.twitter')
IS NOT NULL;
```

Exercise 3: Adding Data to JSON Fields

1. **Goal**: Add a new preference (promotions: true) to each customer's preferences in the JSON Profile column.
2. **Solution**:

```sql
Copy code
UPDATE Customers
SET Profile = JSON_SET(Profile,
'$.preferences.promotions', true);
```

Exercise 4: Checking JSON Array Content

1. **Goal**: Find customers who have purchased specific product categories, stored as an array in the purchases field within Profile.

2. **Table Example**:

```json
{"purchases": ["electronics", "books", "toys"]}
```

3. **Solution**:

```sql
SELECT Name
FROM Customers
WHERE JSON_CONTAINS(Profile, '"electronics"',
'$.purchases');
```

Section 17.6: Common Mistakes and Best Practices for Working with JSON in SQL

1. **Avoid Overusing JSON**: JSON is great for semi-structured data, but using it excessively can make data harder to query and analyze. Only use JSON when you need flexibility for varied data.

2. **Index JSON Columns**: If you frequently query specific fields within JSON columns, consider using JSON indexes (supported in some databases) to improve performance.

3. **Validate JSON Structure**: Ensure that JSON data is well-formed before inserting it into the database. Some databases provide functions to validate JSON, which can prevent errors in querying.

4. **Use JSON Functions Efficiently**: Be mindful that JSON functions like JSON_EXTRACT and JSON_SET can be computationally expensive, so use them only when needed.

5. **Balance JSON and Relational Data**: JSON can be used alongside relational tables, allowing you to store flexible data while keeping core structured data separate for optimized querying.

Section 17.7: Summary and What's Next

In this chapter, you learned how to work with non-relational data in SQL using JSON, storing flexible data structures within relational tables. You explored practical applications like customer profile management, where JSON can store varied information without requiring fixed columns. You also practiced querying and updating JSON data using functions like JSON_EXTRACT and JSON_SET.

In the next chapter, we'll look at **advanced SQL analytics functions**, including window functions and other techniques that allow you to perform sophisticated data analysis within SQL.

CHAPTER 18: SECURITY AND PERMISSIONS

Welcome to Chapter 18! In this chapter, we'll cover **database security** and **permissions management**, critical for protecting data and ensuring that users only access data relevant to their roles. Security measures prevent unauthorized access, reduce risks of data leaks, and help maintain data integrity. By the end of this chapter, you'll understand how to manage user permissions, set up role-based access controls, and apply security best practices, including a real-world example of configuring access for a company's finance database.

Section 18.1: Managing User Permissions and Database Security
SQL databases provide security controls at multiple levels to restrict access to specific users and ensure data integrity. User permissions control **who** can access the database, **what** they can view or modify, and **how** they can interact with the data.

Permissions can be applied at different levels:

1. **Database Level**: Controls access to the entire database (e.g., granting access to HR data but not finance data).

2. **Table Level**: Controls access to specific tables within a database (e.g., allowing access to Salaries but restricting access to ExecutiveSalaries).

3. **Column Level**: Controls access to specific columns within a table (e.g., allowing access to EmployeeID but not SSN).

4. **Row Level**: Some databases support row-level security, controlling access to specific rows within a table based on criteria (e.g., allowing access to data only from specific departments).

Permissions are granted based on **roles** (e.g., Admin, User, Analyst) or **individual users**.

Section 18.2: Granting and Revoking Permissions

SQL provides the **GRANT** and **REVOKE** commands to assign or remove permissions for specific users or roles.

Granting Permissions

The GRANT command is used to provide specific privileges to a user or role.

Syntax:

```sql
Copy code
GRANT privilege ON database.table TO
'username'@'host';
```

- **privilege**: The type of access, such as SELECT, INSERT, UPDATE, or DELETE.
- **database.table**: Specifies the target table or database.
- **username**: The user receiving the permissions.

Example: Granting SELECT permission to the finance_user for the Salaries table.

```sql
Copy code
GRANT SELECT ON CompanyDB.Salaries TO
'finance_user'@'localhost';
```

This command allows `finance_user` to view the `Salaries` table but prevents modifications.

Revoking Permissions

The `REVOKE` command removes previously granted privileges from a user or role.

Syntax:

```sql
Copy code
REVOKE privilege ON database.table FROM
'username'@'host';
```

Example: Revoking `SELECT` permission from the `finance_user`.

```sql
Copy code
REVOKE SELECT ON CompanyDB.Salaries FROM
'finance_user'@'localhost';
```

Now, `finance_user` will no longer have access to view data in the `Salaries` table.

Section 18.3: Real-World Example – Setting Up Access Controls for a Company's Finance Database

Let's consider a scenario where a company's finance database, **FinanceDB**, needs to manage access across different user roles. The finance department has several tables, such as `Salaries`, `Transactions`, and `Budgets`, each containing sensitive data.

Roles and Permissions

1. **Finance Manager**: Full access to all finance data, including modifying and viewing Salaries, Transactions, and Budgets.

2. **Finance Analyst**: Access to view Transactions and Budgets but no access to modify data or view Salaries.

3. **Finance Assistant**: Limited access to view Budgets only.

Step 1: Creating the Roles

If your SQL system supports roles, start by creating the roles:

```sql
Copy code
CREATE ROLE FinanceManager;
CREATE ROLE FinanceAnalyst;
CREATE ROLE FinanceAssistant;
```

Step 2: Granting Permissions to Roles

Assign permissions based on the role requirements:

1. **Finance Manager**: Full access to all tables.

   ```sql
   Copy code
   GRANT ALL PRIVILEGES ON FinanceDB.* TO
   'FinanceManager';
   ```

2. **Finance Analyst**: SELECT access on Transactions and Budgets only.

   ```sql
   Copy code
   GRANT SELECT ON FinanceDB.Transactions TO
   'FinanceAnalyst';
   GRANT SELECT ON FinanceDB.Budgets TO
   'FinanceAnalyst';
   ```

3. **Finance Assistant**: SELECT access on Budgets only.

```sql
Copy code
GRANT SELECT ON FinanceDB.Budgets TO
'FinanceAssistant';
```

Step 3: Assigning Roles to Users

Assign the roles to specific users.

```sql
Copy code
GRANT FinanceManager TO 'john_doe'@'localhost';
GRANT FinanceAnalyst TO 'jane_smith'@'localhost';
GRANT FinanceAssistant TO 'jim_brown'@'localhost';
```

Now each user will have access according to their role without needing individual permissions set on each table.

Section 18.4: Best Practices for Database Security and Permissions

Database security requires careful planning to protect sensitive data and ensure that only authorized users have access. Here are best practices to follow:

1. **Principle of Least Privilege**: Only grant the minimum permissions necessary for each role. For example, if a user only needs to view data, grant SELECT permissions only.

2. **Use Roles Instead of Individual Permissions**: Roles simplify permission management. By assigning permissions to roles rather than individual users, you can more easily manage access as your database grows.

3. **Regularly Review and Audit Permissions**: Periodically check user permissions and roles to ensure that no one has

unnecessary access. This helps maintain security, especially when employees change roles or leave the organization.

4. **Limit Access to Sensitive Data at the Column Level**: For fields like Social Security Numbers or financial details, use column-level permissions where possible. This limits access to sensitive data without restricting access to the entire table.

5. **Implement Row-Level Security When Necessary**: Row-level security can restrict data access based on criteria such as department or region, allowing you to limit data access on a finer level.

6. **Use Encrypted Connections**: For sensitive databases, ensure all connections use SSL or other encryption protocols to protect data during transmission.

Section 18.5: Exercises on Role-Based Permissions and Best Practices

Practice setting up permissions and roles with these exercises.

Exercise 1: Granting Basic Access

1. **Goal**: Grant SELECT permission to a user data_analyst for the SalesData table in the SalesDB database.
2. **Solution**:

```sql
Copy code
GRANT SELECT ON SalesDB.SalesData TO
'data_analyst'@'localhost';
```

Exercise 2: Creating and Assigning a Role

1. **Goal**: Create a role `HRViewer` with `SELECT` permission on the `Employees` and `Payroll` tables in the `HRDB` database and assign it to the user `hr_jane`.
2. **Solution**:

```sql
Copy code
CREATE ROLE HRViewer;
GRANT SELECT ON HRDB.Employees TO HRViewer;
GRANT SELECT ON HRDB.Payroll TO HRViewer;
GRANT HRViewer TO 'hr_jane'@'localhost';
```

Exercise 3: Revoking Access

1. **Goal**: Revoke `UPDATE` permission on the `Inventory` table in the `WarehouseDB` database from the user `warehouse_user`.
2. **Solution**:

```sql
Copy code
REVOKE UPDATE ON WarehouseDB.Inventory FROM
'warehouse_user'@'localhost';
```

Exercise 4: Managing Column-Level Permissions

1. **Goal**: Grant the role `FinanceAssistant` access to only the `BudgetAmount` column in the `Budgets` table.
2. **Solution**: Not all databases support column-level permissions directly. In databases that support it, use syntax like:

```sql
Copy code
GRANT SELECT (BudgetAmount) ON
FinanceDB.Budgets TO 'FinanceAssistant';
```

If column-level permissions aren't supported, create a view with restricted columns and grant access to the view instead.

Section 18.6: Common Mistakes and Best Practices in Managing Security and Permissions

1. **Avoid Granting Excessive Permissions**: Granting ALL PRIVILEGES can open up unnecessary access. Always limit permissions to what's essential for the user's role.

2. **Document Permissions**: Keep a record of permissions granted to each role and user, making it easier to audit and update permissions as requirements change.

3. **Use Views to Limit Column Access**: If column-level permissions aren't available, use views to control access to sensitive columns. Views can filter out or hide specific columns while allowing access to the rest of the table.

4. **Implement Strong Password Policies**: Enforce strong passwords for all database users to reduce the risk of unauthorized access. Many databases allow password complexity policies and expiration settings.

5. **Regularly Update Permissions for Changes in Roles**: As employees change roles or departments, update their permissions promptly to prevent access to data they no longer need.

Section 18.7: Summary and What's Next

In this chapter, you learned about database security and permissions management, including the use of GRANT and REVOKE to manage access at the database, table, and column levels. You saw a real-world example of setting up permissions for a finance database and explored best practices for securing sensitive data. Security is crucial to database management, ensuring data integrity and protecting against unauthorized access.

In the next chapter, we'll explore **SQL performance tuning and optimization**, covering advanced techniques to enhance query efficiency, reduce resource usage, and optimize database performance.

CHAPTER 19: BACKUP, RECOVERY, AND DATA MIGRATION

Welcome to Chapter 19! In this chapter, we'll cover techniques for **database backup, recovery, and migration**. Backing up data and planning for recovery are essential steps in protecting against data loss and ensuring business continuity. We'll also discuss data migration, including a scenario where a local database is migrated to the cloud. By the end of this chapter, you'll understand how to set up database backups, perform recoveries, and migrate data securely and efficiently, along with best practices for data protection and disaster recovery.

Section 19.1: Techniques for Database Backup

Backups are copies of database data, created periodically to protect against data loss from system failure, human error, or natural disasters. There are three main types of backups:

1. **Full Backup**: A complete backup of the entire database, including all tables, data, and configurations. Full backups are typically performed at regular intervals (e.g., weekly or monthly) and serve as a baseline for recovery.

2. **Incremental Backup**: Backs up only the data that has changed since the last backup (full or incremental). Incremental backups are quicker and save storage space, but recovery may require applying multiple backup files.

3. **Differential Backup**: Backs up all changes since the last full backup. Unlike incremental backups, differential backups grow over time but provide a simpler restore process because only the last full backup and the latest differential backup are needed.

Setting Up Backups in SQL

Most SQL databases offer built-in commands and tools for creating backups.

Example: Creating a Full Backup in MySQL

```sql
Copy code
mysqldump -u root -p DatabaseName >
DatabaseName_full_backup.sql
```

This command creates a full backup of `DatabaseName` and saves it to a `.sql` file. You can restore this backup using the `mysql` command.

Section 19.2: Database Recovery

Database recovery involves restoring data from a backup to bring the database back to a consistent state after data loss. The recovery process depends on the backup types available and the tools provided by the database management system.

Recovery Process for Different Backup Types

1. **Full Backup Recovery**: Restore the database from the latest full backup.

2. **Incremental Backup Recovery**: Restore the latest full backup, followed by each incremental backup in sequence.

3. **Differential Backup Recovery**: Restore the latest full backup, followed by the latest differential backup.

Example: Restoring a Full Backup in MySQL

```sql
Copy code
mysql -u root -p DatabaseName <
DatabaseName_full_backup.sql
```

This command restores the `DatabaseName` database from a `.sql` backup file.

Section 19.3: Data Migration Techniques

Data migration involves transferring a database from one system to another, such as moving from a local server to the cloud. A successful migration requires careful planning, testing, and a rollback plan in case of errors.

Common Migration Scenarios:

- **Migrating to the Cloud**: Moving a database from an on-premises environment to a cloud service like AWS RDS, Google Cloud SQL, or Azure SQL.

- **Upgrading Database Versions**: Moving from an older version of a database management system to a newer version.

- **Cross-Platform Migration**: Migrating between different database systems (e.g., MySQL to PostgreSQL).

Steps for Migrating a Local Database to the Cloud

1. **Evaluate Database Compatibility**: Ensure that the cloud service supports your database version and features.
2. **Export Data**: Create a full backup of the local database to capture all data and configurations.
3. **Transfer Data**: Use cloud migration tools or manual transfer (e.g., uploading the backup file to cloud storage).
4. **Import Data into Cloud Database**: Restore the backup on the cloud database instance.
5. **Test and Validate**: Verify data integrity and application compatibility after the migration.
6. **Switch Applications to New Database**: Update application configurations to connect to the cloud database.
7. **Monitor and Optimize**: Monitor performance and make adjustments as needed to optimize cloud resources.

Example: Migrating a MySQL Database to AWS RDS

1. **Step 1**: Export the local MySQL database to an `.sql` file.

```sql
Copy code
mysqldump -u root -p DatabaseName >
DatabaseName.sql
```

2. **Step 2**: Upload the `.sql` file to AWS S3 (or another cloud storage) for transfer.
3. **Step 3**: Connect to the AWS RDS instance and import the database.

```sql
Copy code
mysql -h aws-rds-endpoint -u username -p
DatabaseName < DatabaseName.sql
```

4. **Step 4**: Verify that the data is complete and test all applications using the new database connection.

Section 19.4: Best Practices for Data Protection and Disaster Recovery

1. **Automate Regular Backups**: Set up automated full, incremental, and differential backups as per your needs. Automated backups help prevent human error and ensure that backups are always up-to-date.

2. **Store Backups in Multiple Locations**: Use redundant backup locations, including offsite and cloud storage, to ensure that data is recoverable in case of regional disasters.

3. **Encrypt Backup Files**: Use encryption to protect sensitive data in backups, especially when storing backups in cloud storage or transporting them offsite.

4. **Test Backup and Recovery Processes**: Regularly test both backup and recovery procedures to ensure they work as expected. Run test recoveries in a staging environment to confirm data integrity.

5. **Monitor Backup Logs**: Backup tools often provide logs that record the success or failure of each backup. Regularly review these logs to catch any issues early.

6. **Use Managed Cloud Backup Services**: Many cloud providers offer managed backup services with automated scheduling, incremental backups, and secure storage. These services simplify backup management and reduce administrative overhead.

7. **Document the Disaster Recovery Plan**: Maintain documentation for backup and recovery procedures, including roles and responsibilities, step-by-step recovery instructions, and contact information for key personnel.

Section 19.5: Exercises on Backup, Recovery, and Migration

Try these exercises to practice backup, recovery, and migration techniques.

Exercise 1: Creating a Full Backup

1. **Goal**: Create a full backup of a local database called `InventoryDB`.
2. **Solution**:

```sql
Copy code
mysqldump -u root -p InventoryDB >
InventoryDB_full_backup.sql
```

Exercise 2: Restoring a Full Backup

1. **Goal**: Restore the `InventoryDB` database from the `InventoryDB_full_backup.sql` backup file.
2. **Solution**:

```sql
Copy code
mysql -u root -p InventoryDB <
InventoryDB_full_backup.sql
```

Exercise 3: Automating Incremental Backups

1. **Goal**: Set up automated incremental backups for a MySQL database. (Hint: Use a scheduling tool such as `cron` in Unix-based systems to run incremental backups periodically.)
2. **Solution**: Create a shell script to perform incremental backups and use `cron` to schedule it. Example script:

```bash
Copy code
# incremental_backup.sh
mysqldump -u root -p --single-transaction --
quick --lock-tables=false DatabaseName >
DatabaseName_incremental_$(date +%F).sql
```

Schedule it in `cron`:

```bash
Copy code
0 2 * * * /path/to/incremental_backup.sh
```

Exercise 4: Migrating a Local Database to the Cloud

1. **Goal**: Plan a migration of a local MySQL database to a cloud service (e.g., AWS RDS or Google Cloud SQL).
2. **Solution**: Follow these steps:
   1. Export the local MySQL database.
   2. Transfer the backup file to the cloud.

3. Import the backup into the cloud database instance.

4. Test and validate data integrity in the cloud database.

Section 19.6: Common Mistakes and Best Practices in Backup, Recovery, and Migration

1. **Not Testing Backups Regularly**: A backup is only useful if it's restorable. Regularly test your backups in a staging environment to ensure data is intact and recovery processes are reliable.

2. **Neglecting Encryption for Sensitive Backups**: Always encrypt backup files containing sensitive data to prevent unauthorized access if they're exposed.

3. **Ignoring Backup Logs**: Backup failures can go unnoticed if logs aren't monitored. Set up automated alerts for any backup failures to take timely action.

4. **Relying on a Single Backup Location**: Store backups in multiple locations, including offsite or cloud storage, to mitigate the risk of losing data in a regional disaster.

5. **Skipping Migration Testing**: During migration, test the new database environment thoroughly for performance, compatibility, and data integrity. Validate data with checksums or row counts to ensure nothing is lost in the migration.

6. **Failing to Document the Recovery Plan**: Document every aspect of your recovery plan, including contact information, backup schedules, recovery procedures, and testing schedules. This ensures efficient and reliable recovery when needed.

Section 19.7: Summary and What's Next

In this chapter, you learned about techniques for database backup, recovery, and migration, covering different backup types, the recovery process, and key steps for migrating data to a new environment like the cloud. You also reviewed best practices to protect data and ensure reliable disaster recovery.

In the next chapter, we'll explore **SQL monitoring and performance tuning** to optimize database performance, focusing on query efficiency, resource utilization, and identifying potential bottlenecks.

CHAPTER 20: SQL IN THE REAL WORLD – BEST PRACTICES AND TIPS

Congratulations on reaching Chapter 20! This final chapter brings together the best practices you've learned throughout this book, along with practical tips for applying SQL in real-world scenarios. SQL skills go beyond syntax mastery; they include writing optimized, readable code, handling data efficiently, and maintaining database reliability as it scales. By the end of this chapter, you'll have a toolkit of strategies to keep your SQL skills sharp and practical advice for tackling challenges in real-world database environments.

Section 20.1: Best Practices for Query Optimization, Data Handling, and Code Readability

To become proficient in SQL, it's essential to write efficient, maintainable, and scalable queries. Here are best practices that help achieve these goals.

1. Query Optimization

Optimizing queries ensures that your database can handle large datasets, complex joins, and frequent transactions without sacrificing performance.

- **Use Indexes Wisely**: Index frequently queried columns and avoid over-indexing to keep write operations efficient.

- **Filter Data Early**: Use WHERE clauses, JOIN filters, and subqueries to narrow down results as early as possible in a query.

- **Avoid SELECT * in Production**: Only select the columns you need rather than retrieving all columns. This reduces data transfer time and resource usage.

- **Use Joins Efficiently**: Minimize the number of joins in a query by designing tables thoughtfully and using INNER JOIN over OUTER JOIN where possible.

- **Limit Subqueries**: Whenever possible, use joins instead of subqueries, as they are often more efficient and easier to optimize.

Example: Using column-specific queries and indexing.

```sql
Copy code
SELECT CustomerID, Name, Email
FROM Customers
WHERE Status = 'Active'
AND SignupDate > '2022-01-01';
```

In this example, only the required columns (CustomerID, Name, Email) are selected, and filters are applied to restrict the dataset.

2. Data Handling and Security

Ensuring data integrity and security is crucial, especially in shared database environments.

- **Implement ACID Transactions**: Use transactions for operations that require atomicity, consistency, isolation, and durability, such as financial transactions or bulk updates.

- **Enforce Constraints**: Use primary keys, foreign keys, and unique constraints to maintain data consistency and prevent duplicate or invalid records.

- **Use Parameterized Queries**: Avoid SQL injection attacks by using parameterized queries instead of dynamically building SQL statements.

- **Set Appropriate Permissions**: Limit access to tables and databases by setting permissions based on the user's role, following the principle of least privilege.

Example: Using a transaction to ensure consistent data updates.

```sql
Copy code
START TRANSACTION;

UPDATE Accounts
SET Balance = Balance - 500
WHERE AccountID = 101;

UPDATE Accounts
SET Balance = Balance + 500
WHERE AccountID = 202;

COMMIT;
```

This transaction ensures that either both updates occur, or neither does, preventing inconsistencies in account balances.

3. Code Readability and Maintainability

Readable SQL code is essential for collaboration, debugging, and future maintenance.

- **Use Descriptive Aliases**: Use meaningful aliases for table names or columns to make your queries easier to understand.

- **Organize SQL Statements**: Use indentation, line breaks, and uppercase keywords (e.g., SELECT, WHERE, JOIN) to improve readability.

- **Comment Complex Queries**: Add comments to explain non-intuitive logic, especially for complex joins, subqueries, or calculations.

- **Modularize with Views and CTEs**: Use **views** and **common table expressions (CTEs)** for complex queries. These structures make code modular, reusable, and more readable.

Example: Using a CTE for readability in a report query.

```sql
Copy code
WITH RecentOrders AS (
    SELECT OrderID, CustomerID, OrderDate
    FROM Orders
    WHERE OrderDate > DATE_SUB(CURDATE(), INTERVAL 30 DAY)
)
SELECT Customers.Name, RecentOrders.OrderID,
RecentOrders.OrderDate
FROM Customers
JOIN RecentOrders ON Customers.CustomerID =
RecentOrders.CustomerID;
```

Using the `RecentOrders` CTE makes it clear that the query is focused on orders from the last 30 days.

Section 20.2: Real-World Scenarios – Scaling Databases and Error-Free Reporting

SQL is versatile, but real-world demands introduce challenges that require more than basic skills. Here's how SQL best practices help solve practical issues.

Scenario 1: Scaling a Database for Growth

As databases grow, performance issues can emerge due to larger datasets, more users, or complex queries. Here's how to scale effectively:

- **Partition Large Tables**: For very large tables, use partitioning to split them into smaller, manageable segments based on a key (e.g., by date). This reduces query times and optimizes storage.

- **Optimize Indexes**: Periodically review and update indexes. As data changes, some indexes may become fragmented or less effective, so monitoring and optimizing indexes is crucial.

- **Consider Read Replicas**: If your database supports it, use read replicas to handle read-heavy workloads without affecting primary database performance.

- **Use Connection Pooling**: Set up connection pools to handle high user concurrency without overwhelming the database with too many connections.

Example: Partitioning a large `Sales` table by year.

```sql
Copy code
CREATE TABLE Sales_2022 PARTITION OF Sales
FOR VALUES IN (2022);
```
Partitioning by year reduces the query time when searching within specific time ranges.

Scenario 2: Creating Accurate, Error-Free Reports

Generating accurate reports often requires consolidating data across multiple tables, handling missing data, and performing calculations.

- **Use Window Functions for Aggregations**: Window functions allow you to calculate running totals, averages, and ranks across rows without complex subqueries.

- **Handle NULLs Explicitly**: Use COALESCE to replace NULL values with default values or labels in reports.

- **Ensure Consistent Time Zones and Units**: When handling date-time data or measurements across regions, standardize time zones and units for consistency in reports.

- **Automate Regular Reports**: Use stored procedures or scheduled queries to generate recurring reports and reduce manual effort.

Example: Using window functions to calculate cumulative sales totals.

```sql
Copy code
SELECT CustomerID, OrderDate, Amount,
       SUM(Amount) OVER (PARTITION BY CustomerID
ORDER BY OrderDate) AS CumulativeTotal
FROM Orders;
```

This query calculates a cumulative total for each customer over time, without needing complex subqueries.

Section 20.3: Final Tips on Mastering SQL and Keeping Skills Sharp

Mastering SQL requires continuous learning and adapting to new challenges. Here are some tips to keep your skills up-to-date and deepen your understanding.

1. **Practice with Real Datasets**: Work with open datasets to practice querying, optimizing, and analyzing real-world data. This experience helps you apply theoretical concepts practically.

2. **Experiment with Advanced SQL Features**: Explore advanced SQL features like window functions, recursive queries, and complex joins. Mastering these techniques prepares you for handling sophisticated data requirements.

3. **Stay Updated with SQL Innovations**: Many database systems evolve regularly, adding new features or optimizations. Keep an eye on updates for the database

systems you use, such as MySQL, PostgreSQL, SQL Server, or Oracle.

4. **Optimize Queries with EXPLAIN**: Use EXPLAIN to analyze how queries are executed and identify potential bottlenecks. This tool provides insights into indexing needs, join performance, and execution order.

5. **Collaborate and Review Code**: Work with teammates to review and discuss SQL code. Peer review enhances your understanding, exposes you to new techniques, and improves code quality.

6. **Document Your Queries**: Keep a library of your commonly used queries, optimized patterns, and snippets, and include comments for future reference. This practice is especially valuable for complex queries that require multiple steps or transformations.

7. **Leverage Online Resources**: SQL communities, forums, and online resources like Stack Overflow, SQLZoo, and Khan Academy's SQL courses provide solutions, challenges, and new ideas to explore.

Section 20.4: Summary and Conclusion

In this final chapter, we reviewed SQL best practices for optimizing queries, managing data securely, and writing readable code. You explored real-world scenarios like scaling databases and generating accurate reports, and gathered tips on how to continue developing your SQL skills. From efficient querying to mastering data security, these practices help you handle SQL challenges in any environment.

Congratulations on completing this journey! By mastering SQL's core concepts and advanced features, you're well-prepared to manage data effectively, optimize performance, and contribute meaningfully to data-driven projects. Keep practicing, exploring, and building on your SQL knowledge, and you'll find that SQL opens doors to a world of data insights and opportunities.

SQL Mastery: A Comprehensive Summary

SQL, or Structured Query Language, is the foundation for managing and interacting with data in relational databases. Through this summary, we'll cover the critical concepts, best practices, and practical applications that are essential for effectively using SQL in real-world scenarios.

Chapter 1-5: SQL Basics and Core Commands

The journey into SQL begins with understanding its core structure and the commands that form the backbone of querying. SQL is built on commands such as SELECT, INSERT, UPDATE, and DELETE, which enable you to retrieve, modify, and manage data within tables.

- **Basic Commands**:
  - SELECT retrieves data from tables.
  - INSERT adds new rows.
  - UPDATE modifies existing rows.
  - DELETE removes rows.

These fundamental commands allow users to interact with databases and perform essential operations. Additionally, using clauses like WHERE for filtering, ORDER BY for sorting, and GROUP BY for data aggregation enhances the utility of basic queries.

Real-World Application: Consider a company needing to generate a list of customers who have recently signed up. A SELECT query with WHERE and ORDER BY clauses would efficiently generate this report.

Chapter 6-10: Advanced Querying Techniques

Advanced querying techniques build on SQL's basic commands and focus on more complex data retrieval and manipulation. Key techniques covered include joins, aggregations, and conditional filtering:

- **Joins**: Joins (e.g., INNER JOIN, LEFT JOIN) allow data retrieval across multiple tables based on related columns, facilitating comprehensive data insights without redundancy.
- **Aggregation Functions**: Functions like SUM, COUNT, AVG, MIN, and MAX calculate aggregated values across rows, often used alongside GROUP BY to organize data.
- **Filtering with Clauses**: Advanced filtering techniques use operators and clauses like IN, LIKE, BETWEEN, and IS NULL to refine query results.

Example: Analyzing sales data by product category involves joining tables, aggregating total sales, and filtering results to display only top-selling products.

Chapter 11-15: Data Management and Performance Optimization

As databases grow in complexity, efficient data management and optimization become essential. SQL provides functions for handling dates and times, creating views for simplified data access, and managing data through transactions and indexing:

- **Date and Time Functions**: SQL's date functions (e.g., CURRENT_DATE, DATEDIFF, DATE_ADD) make it easy to perform calculations with date-based data, such as tracking order timelines.

- **Views**: Views allow you to save complex queries as virtual tables. They streamline data access for non-technical users and enhance data security by controlling column visibility.

- **Transactions**: Transactions are essential for maintaining data consistency and reliability, especially in operations requiring multiple steps. Using BEGIN, COMMIT, and ROLLBACK ensures that operations are completed fully or not at all.

- **Indexing**: Indexes improve query performance by allowing the database to locate data quickly, reducing query time. However, indexes increase storage requirements and can slow down write operations, so they should be used thoughtfully.

Practical Scenario: In e-commerce, date functions track the status of orders, and views can provide non-technical staff access to relevant order details without exposing sensitive customer data.

Chapter 16-19: Data Integrity, Security, and Backup
Ensuring data integrity, security, and backup is crucial for maintaining database reliability. These chapters cover techniques for data normalization, permissions, and disaster recovery:

- **Normalization**: Organizing tables through normalization (1NF, 2NF, 3NF) reduces redundancy and improves data integrity. By structuring tables logically, databases become easier to maintain and more efficient to query.
- **Security and Permissions**: SQL includes robust permission management tools (GRANT and REVOKE) that control access based on user roles. Role-based permissions restrict data access, allowing users only the minimum necessary access.
- **Backup and Recovery**: Regular backups protect against data loss. Full, incremental, and differential backups each have specific use cases and recovery processes. Data migration processes ensure a seamless transfer of databases, such as moving from on-premises to cloud environments.

Example: A finance team may require read-only access to transaction data. Role-based permissions grant only the necessary permissions while restricting access to other sensitive data, such as customer contact information.

Chapter 20: Real-World Best Practices for SQL Mastery

This chapter consolidates SQL best practices that are essential for working with real-world databases efficiently and securely.

1. Query Optimization:

Optimizing queries ensures that they run efficiently, even on large datasets. Avoid `SELECT *` in favor of selecting specific columns, use indexing strategically, and apply filters early in the query to reduce data volume quickly. Modularizing complex queries with views or Common Table Expressions (CTEs) also improves readability and maintainability.

Example: Instead of `SELECT *`, selecting specific columns reduces the amount of data retrieved, speeding up query execution and reducing resource usage.

2. Data Handling and Security:

Protecting data integrity and security is a top priority. Use ACID transactions to ensure that complex operations are completed consistently, enforce foreign key constraints to maintain referential integrity, and implement secure data handling practices such as parameterized queries to avoid SQL injection attacks.

Example: ACID-compliant transactions are critical for financial applications where all changes must either be fully applied or rolled back in case of error.

3. Code Readability and Maintainability:

Readable and maintainable SQL code promotes collaboration, eases debugging, and simplifies future updates. Descriptive aliases, consistent formatting, and comments clarify code structure and purpose. Using modular structures like CTEs or views for complex queries ensures better organization and readability.

Example: Using aliases like `cust` for `Customers` and `ord` for `Orders` makes queries clearer, especially in complex joins.

Real-World SQL Applications and Tips for Continued Learning

SQL's applications are vast, from powering e-commerce platforms to managing customer data in CRM systems. Here are some real-world applications and tips for mastering SQL over time.

Scaling Databases:

As datasets grow, maintaining performance requires additional strategies beyond indexing. Partitioning divides large tables based on criteria (e.g., date) to speed up queries within specific ranges, and read replicas allow multiple instances to handle read-heavy workloads.

Example: An online retailer might partition a `Sales` table by year, reducing the amount of data accessed when querying sales for a specific year.

Creating Error-Free Reports:

Data accuracy is critical in reporting. Window functions and aggregate functions help calculate metrics like cumulative sales or rankings without needing complex subqueries. Using `COALESCE` to handle `NULL` values, validating date formats, and standardizing units or time zones ensures reports remain consistent.

Example: Generating a quarterly sales report with cumulative totals for each region can be done with window functions, reducing query complexity and improving accuracy.

Final Tips for SQL Mastery and Continuous Improvement

SQL skills improve with practice and consistent learning. Here are tips to help keep your SQL knowledge sharp:

1. **Practice with Real Data**: Working on open datasets allows you to apply SQL skills to real-world data, enhancing your understanding of performance and optimization challenges.

2. **Learn Advanced Techniques**: Delve into advanced SQL features like window functions, recursive queries, and indexing strategies to improve your ability to handle complex requirements.

3. **Keep Up with Updates**: Database systems evolve frequently, so stay informed about new features and optimizations in the database systems you use, such as MySQL, PostgreSQL, SQL Server, or Oracle.

4. **Optimize Using EXPLAIN**: Use the EXPLAIN command to analyze query execution plans and optimize performance by understanding how SQL processes each step.

5. **Collaborate and Review Code**: Code reviews encourage collaborative learning, expose you to new techniques, and help you understand best practices for efficient and readable SQL code.

6. **Document Queries**: Keep a library of your most useful queries, optimizations, and insights, along with comments explaining complex logic. This practice is especially helpful when dealing with recurring queries and maintaining consistency in complex queries.

7. **Leverage Online Resources**: SQL communities, forums, and resources like SQLZoo, Stack Overflow, and Khan Academy provide challenges, insights, and opportunities to deepen your understanding.

SQL is more than just a language for querying databases; it's a powerful tool for organizing, managing, and analyzing data. Throughout these chapters, you've covered essential SQL commands, advanced data manipulation techniques, strategies for managing performance, and tips for creating secure, reliable systems.

By following best practices in query optimization, data security, and code readability, and by applying SQL in real-world scenarios, you'll be well-prepared to handle the challenges of managing data effectively.

From the fundamentals of `SELECT` statements to advanced indexing strategies, normalization, and data security measures, you've gained a robust foundation to work confidently with SQL. Keep practicing, stay curious, and remember that each new query or optimization is an opportunity to deepen your understanding and refine your skills. With continued learning and experience, SQL will remain a valuable and versatile skill in your data toolkit.